THE LAND OF
GREEN TEA

COL. WYNDHAM BAKER

THE LAND OF GREEN TEA

Letters and Adventures of
Colonel C.L. Baker of the
Madras Artillery
1834–1850

(In India and the First Chinese Opium War)

EDITED BY

PAMELA MASEFIELD

UNICORN PRESS

Dedicated to my mother, Gladwys Wyndham Masefield
and
to my husband
Llewellyn Arthur Hugh-Jones O.B.E.
and The Order of the Nile.

First published in the United Kingdom in 1995 by Unicorn Press, 21 Afghan Road, SW11 2QD

ISBN 0 906290 11 2

Typesetting and origination by Alan Sutton Publishing Limited.
Printed in Great Britain by WBC Limited, Bridgend, Mid Glamorgan.

Contents

Acknowledgements

The British Museum. For an invaluable list of books.

The India Office Library. Miss E.C.D. Hoffman.

The National Maritime Museum, Greenwich. The Librarian and his assistants and The Keeper of the Prints.

The Tate Gallery. Miss Mary Charnot.

The Percival David Foundation of Chinese Art. Miss B.W.D. Martin.

The Berry-Hill Galleries, New York, U.S.A.

Mr. Douglas Blackwood of William Blackwood & Sons Ltd., who published two extracts of the letters in his magazines of July and August 1964, which gave me much encouragement.

Matheson & Co. Ltd., of London E.C.3. Mr. Alan Reid.

Messrs. Brown Son & Ferguson Ltd. of Glasgow, S.I.

Encyclopaedia Britannica

Also with deep gratitude to Col. J.K. Stanford of the Indian Civil Service, without whose help, advice and kindly criticism these Letters would never have become a book.

List of Illustrations

The Baker Family

Frances Baker, born April 14th, 1773, died August 15th, 1840.
   Rector of Coombe Bissett, and Wylye, Wiltshire.
Elizabeth Colton, born May 24th, 1774.
   Married September 23rd, 1800 at Shrivenham.

Their Children

Frances Edward Baker,	born Sept. 1801–67 at Salisbury.
Elizabeth Sarah Baker,	” Aug. 1802–76 ” ”
Augusta Baker,	” Nov. 1803 ” ”
Emily Maryanne Baker,	” June 1805–22 ” ”
George Edward Baker, (Solicitor)	” May 1807–91 ” ”
Louisa Margaret,[1]	Oct. 1808–1942 at Coombe Bisset near Salisbury
Georgina Baker, Isobel Octavia Baker	” March 1812 at ” ”
Edward Baker,	” March 1812 at ” ”
Julia Mary Baker,	” Sept. 1813–46 ” ”
Harriett Augusta Baker	” March 1816–1917 at Haslemere
Wyndham Charles Leopold	” **Dec. 1817–1875 at Coombe Bisset**
Isabella Octavia Baker[2]	” Feb. 1821 at Fifehead House in Dorsetshire

1. *Known as "Aunt Louie", the mother of my beloved godmother, Miss Marjorie Brodie. – Editor.*
2. *My maternal great-grandmother. – Editor.*

Foreword
and the Story of the Letters

I wish here to acknowledge my gratitude to the late Mrs. Widdicombe, who, when I met her in 1938 at Torquay, was Col. Wyndham Baker's only surviving daughter. From her kind letters, co-operations, and occasional tea-parties, are due the few stories I have been able to collect together, of one who was much loved by his family. She also let me have the family portrait photographed (Frontispiece), which is now in possession of her youngest daughter Mrs. Foster of Bath. Mrs. Foster wrote of her mother that she was Wyndham's youngest child, and had inherited his bright coloured red hair. In her life she was full of charm and very good company, so it seems she was a chip off the old block! That she was popular and debonnaire is borne out by the fact that she married three times.

Perhaps today we miss something that our ancestors held dear, namely the welding together of all members of a family, however large, and Wyndham was the eleventh or twelfth child out of 12 (or 13, we are not sure). In his letters he is anxious for the welfare of all his family, not only of his favourite brothers and sisters. He sometimes enquires tactfully after Edward, who rarely if ever wrote and was said to be the black sheep of the family, but he does it carefully, knowing that the subject may be painful and a cause of anxiety to his parents. Sister Harriett is never left out, and she lived to trouble her relations for 101 years; but it is due to my great-grand-Aunt Harriett's patience and care in guarding the letters, that we have any knowledge of her brother Wyndham and his doings at all. (At my grandmother Mrs. Sanders' death, the letters were found in bundles

Isaobel Julia Brodie My Grandmother (Ed.) & Wyndham's niece known as "the Belle of Warwickshire" at Hunt-Balls because of her lily-white skin – suntan was not considered the fashion in those days.

tied up with blue ribbon in her desk.) Mr. Blackwood alluded to me as Wyndham's "great-grand-niece" when he published two extracts from the letters in his magazines of July and August in 1964. I do not know if he was correct or not, but he was the first to encourage me. Great-aunt Harriett copied out sheets of the letters with Mama and they were generally sewn together and circulated round the family. It was due to my dear old grandmother (née Isobel Julia Brodie), daughter of Wyndham's sister Isobel Octavia Baker, that we owe the fact that the letters were never thrown away. She was a grand old Victorian tartar, bullying her own daughters with cold baths before breakfast and piano practice; lipstick, that sign of Jezebel was taboo! Also if men visitors wanted to smoke they had to go to the library or the garden. But in her youth with a fair white skin, of which she was inordinately proud, she had been known as "the Belle of Warwickshire" at hunt balls. I think my mother was her favourite daughter as she was the one chosen to be painted, actually sketched in pastel, and she certainly had a soft spot for this grand-daughter, who often used to stay with her. However, it was when I was older and earning my living in London, that I really enjoyed and savoured life at Pine Ridge in Haslemere, where I snatched brief holidays between typing jobs that I never really liked.

It was delicious to be a very welcome visitor and lie in bed of a morning, waiting for Mary's gentle "tap-tap" on the door. Mary, the good old-fashioned housemaid, with her prim little bun and crisp white cap and apron. It was always; "Good Morning Miss Pamela and here's your hot water!" and she would put it down by the basin and cold water jug covered with roses, while she drew back the curtains and remarked on the weather, leaving behind her the early morning tea and thin bread-and-butter to greet the morning.

The pigeons would be cooing on the roof and scuttering and making that busy gurgling sound that was always associated with Pine Ridge; and I would stretch luxuriously and know that there was no hurry about breakfast and anyway it would all be cooked for me. There was no need to dash for an early bus to the office clutching a sandwich; just peace – infinite peace and the pigeons, and a nice inner feeling of warmth and well-being as I sipped my tea and a feeling of laziness spreading through every limb.

Dear old Granny; somehow we had a fellow-feeling – perhaps it was because most of her family ran her down, and I was rather a lump and not very clever – but we did not grate on each other; perhaps she loved me, I do not know, or perhaps she was sorry for me – at any rate we were just happy together!

In the evening "Arthur" would come in bearing the lamp aloft, which was always lit after dinner. It was almost as large as himself. Arthur had been the Boots, then the pantry-boy, and lastly the so-called butler. Then he married Alice, the cook – the most convenient arrangement – and they had been given a little flat over the disused stables (in my grandfather's time they had a coach-and-four and all the girls were brought up to ride and follow hounds). Arthur had snow-white hair and ruddy cheeks and a cheery smile, and he was ever so short as though something had suddenly made him stop growing at about 14, but latterly he was a bit slow in his steps. When he had cleared the table and left, Granny and I pulled the old leather chairs round with their backs to the light, and put on our ear-phones and, joy of joy, we listened to the news in the early days of radio!

I am writing a little now about my old home – although it has nothing to do with Wyndham – it is for my son and those who come after him. It was called The Knapp, Ledbury, in the county of Herefordshire. My father's forbears had always been the solicitors of Ledbury – Masefield and Masefield.

On the other side of the road was The Knapp Lane, which led up to a quarry, and at the bottom of the Lane was Mrs. Crease's cottage, my mother's washerwoman. She washed one day a week and ironed the next day with those heavy irons on a coal-burning stove, just like Mrs. Tiggy-Winkle used to. Mrs. Crease had reddish-purple everlasting peas in her garden which I much admired and I vowed to myself that when I had a garden I would grow them.

The Knapp was a black-and-white house with three acres of lovely garden, field and pond. The pond had a little wooden walk-way across one corner where we used to talk to the lily-white ducks, who sometimes misbehaved and laid their eggs in the water (later an addled egg would bob up and down on the far side of the pond). It was memorable to me as the place where I saw my first fairy – just a flash of blue – though in more mature years I had to admit that I

Gladwys Wyndham Sanders my Mother and Wyndham's god-daughter.

believe it was a blue dragonfly!

The house was built on a high point, and after two round beds of flowers, tulips in season, the ground sloped down to a grass tennis court at the bottom with fences at each end covered with rambler roses. Behind the left fence was my mother's picking place, where lots of bulbs were planted where she went to find flowers for the house and we had our sand-heap. There was a fence covered with ivy there where I found my first wren's nest. Jenny Wren had made a lovely round ball of moss with a tiny hole at one side where she hid lots of minute eggs.

Down the first bank from the house lots of aconites sprouted in spring, yellow flowers with green toby collars which I have loved ever since and at the bottom of the bank someone had put an old round millstone where we had tea in summer. However, the joy of our lives, my brother John and I, were two old yew trees grown together of enormous girth which we used to climb. We named the branches Box B, the Mistress Squeeze, the Flying Outlauncher, and of course the best thing about it was that if we did not want to come down, no nurse or young governess could possibly get us down. It was a dear old tree, a cool shady place in summer and a sheltered place in winter where we had our swing and gave sermons on stilts. High up in the tree was a land of its own for my brother and me, a strange quiet place full of yew leaves and yew berries, and the dirty brown bark which was pink underneath – a strange quiet place as high as the birds. It was peaceful up there and no one knew where you were, though they probably guessed!

It was my mother, Mrs. Reginald Masefield, who rescued the Letters on my Granny's death, when with many years accumulation of lumber they very nearly found their way to the bonfire. She saved them for me at my special request, and it is to her, one of the bravest of women, that I dedicate Wyndham's story, one more link with that past which is rapidly fading. I also dedicate it to my husband, the most important person in my life who, while I sit typing, manfully does the shopping! Between Wyndham and his mother, as is sometimes the case between mother and son, there existed a spiritual bond that neither time nor distance could sever. There is something heartrending in the story of this mother's love for a son who is far

away, separated from all he loves, and when he did come home with
his wife after 19 years abroad, she was no longer alive.

We gather from his family that Wyndham had an extraordinarily
loveable personality as everyone liked him, perhaps because he was so
witty, clever, and above all so kind-hearted, never thinking unkind
things of others.

Mrs. Widdicome wrote: "Father had very bright golden-red hair
and blue eyes, which looks so unreal when painted (real carrots), and
we all had it too. My enemies said I dyed my hair, but when my
children had the same they retracted a bit.

"Father always wore an eye-glass and had very merry eyes. As a
child I adored him, he was always playing practical jokes on
everyone.

"Yes, he was a captain when he married my mother, but he died in
1875, so did not live long after he retired to enjoy that home life
which he had so longed for and written about so often.

"He was only 58 when he died, from the effects of being tossed by a
bull on the Common at Bath. It was running at a child and he put out
his arms to save the infant, so the bull tossed him instead and as he
was over 6ft. 3ins. tall, he was badly gored and never got over it,
dying a year after to the day."

"Everything comes to him who waits," we are told, and so his
mother waited – invariably the woman's part – through 17 long
years, always hoping, praying that she might see the day of his return.
But she died too soon as he did not come home till 1864, after 30
years abroad in India and China.

And then when he did return with his wife to enjoy a home, which,
as his mother said, "is after all the real bliss of a life that will lead to
Heaven," he only lived 11 more years.

Mrs. Widdicombe wrote: "My mother died in Cheltenham. The
little house was often pointed out to me by Aunt Harriett Baker,
Father's sister, who lived to be 101!

"You know of course that Father brought home a native servant
named 'Cartee,' a Madrasee, who he was devoted to, and who had
saved his life in one of the Chinese Riots, and died in Father's house
at Green Park, Bath.

"I remember quite well the scene of Cartee's christening. He had

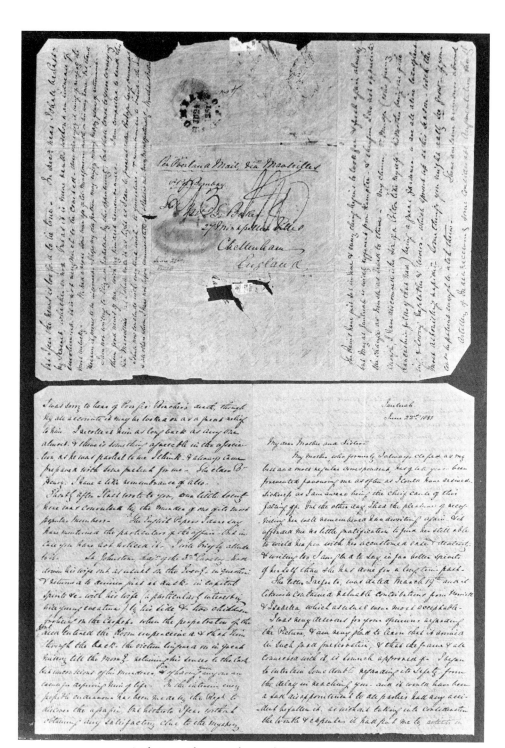

A photograph copy of one of the original letters.

been told by Father that the doctors said he would not live, and Father had offered to send him back to Madras to his own people, hoping the heat might help him, but Cartee said: 'Sahib, your God is my God, I will stay with you,' so he was christened in the dining-room at Green Park and Father was his Godfather.

"I can see it all now, the row of servants that came in with Cartee, the old Parson and Father at the end of the table, where Cartee was christened from a big silver mug with such joy on his face. Father was with him when he died soon after and he was buried at Tellisford."

The Knapp at Ledbury (my old home), had some unusual fruit trees in the field, such as Perry Pears (now Babycham), crab apples on which mistletoe conveniently grew, and a lovely old walnut tree (alas I have never had a fresh walnut since – never mind their brown stain from the outer green shell; perhaps the Druids used it with their woad?).

To go back to the house, the word "to knapp" was to flake off bits of flint to fashion Norman arrow heads. The church in Ledbury is Norman and the largest parish church in Great Britain (I used to think it very gloomy sitting through hour-long sermons and the Litany). The famous bit of old Ledbury is the cobbled Church Lane (where I think my uncle must have had his idea for "The Widow in the Bye Street"). It led from the Market Place on stilts to the church and the rectory where King Charles is supposed to have hidden in the stables after the Battle of Ledbury. In my early days a red climbing rose grew over the drawing room window of the house and a milkish-white climbing rose grew round the dining room window on the left and made its way above to our nursery window where I could pick it. A fine old cabbagy rose with a bit of scent, "Gloire de Dijon;" I have it in my garden doing well today.

The Masefield Family tree goes back to "1066 and all that" to a Chauncy de Chauncy who came over with William, as you will see if you look in a book called "Thierry's Norman Conquest". My father was very interested in family trees, whereas my half-Welsh husband was not; he used to say, "I am descended from ap Adam ap God".

Since Mr. Douglas Blackwood published two instalments in his magazine in July and August 1964, I re-edited the letters afresh with the help and advice of J.K. Stanford of the Indian Civil Service, soldier and well-known author of "The Twelfth," and "Ladies in the Sun," etc. He kindly went over all the material from India, especially the chapters on Madras, Secunderabad, and Kurnoul, and if it had not been for him repeatedly saying: "I am sure you have a book here if we can only edit it properly," I should have given up the unequal struggle long ago.

I was Pamela Masefield then, living at Grey Gables, Thurlestone in South Devon, my mother's home.

September 12th, 1965.

Early Days at Addiscombe

Addiscombe was the East India Company's Training College, founded in 1809. Wyndham in one of his letters to his mother says: "do come and visit me at Addiscombe, such lovely country round here!" Now it is in the heart of Croydon.

The Elizabethan house was inherited by one William Draper, son-in-law of the celebrated diarist John Evelyn, through his Aunt, Lady Temple. Later it was sold in 1809 by a Mr. Radcliffe to the Hon. East India Co. (I have a lovely picture of the cadets drilling in a field along with a herd of cows.)

The cadets lived on a spartan diet and each paid £30 half-yearly to cover the cost of "books, mathematical instruments, stationery, pocket money (2/6 per week) washing, cloathes & medical attendance."

By 1826 Addiscombe owned 30 acres and new buildings were built to house 150 cadets, a bakehouse, dairy, laundry and brewery; their basic clothes were given them and mortars supplied. "1/9 was allowed for Cadet's meals, and 1/6 for servants per day", so they seemed to live mainly on bread, butter and cheese, with beer at lunch. Smoking was not allowed and considered "a filthy and pernicious habit", but they found ways of having a quiet smoke in hidden corners of the grounds. Jonathan Cape was their celebrated master for 39 years.

Unfortunately only three letters survive from the young Wyndham Baker written from Addiscombe, and the only thing he seems to tell us about it is that: "it is a mile from Croydon in beautiful country."

It was an historic old house with its ceilings covered with gods and goddesses, and one wonders what the early cadets thought of Pan surprising the nymph Syrinx, etc. Evelyn, the diarist, mentions it in 1703 as being of "solid and good architecture." It then belonged to his son-in-law, who afterwards sold it to Mr. Radcliffe of the Hon.

The Military Seminar at Addiscombe c. 1829

Scene from Nature drawn on Stone by Henry Perry. Reproduced by kind permission of the National Army Museum.

East India Co. The old house had been associated with the great Pitt and his friends who held carousals there, and from Major Broadfoot's article in Blackwood's Magazine of 1893, and Col. H.M. Vibart's book, "Addiscombe, its Heroes and Men of Note," one hears numerous anecdotes of the early cadets' spartan life which also had its lighter side.

The story I liked the most was the one of the "black putty bars"; these were removed at night after lock-up to enable the cadets to break bounds, and replaced by day. The matter came to a head one time when the nearest town had a fire in the middle of the night which was put out by the cadets, and the story leaked into the local press, which made the governors of the Military Seminary (as it was then called), sit up and take notice, but they never spotted the black putty bars.

One of Wyndham Baker's first letters to have been kept: written to his father in a childish handwriting.

Letter addressed to:
The Rev. Frances Baker,
Wylye Rectory,
Near Salisbury.,

Dec. 2nd, 1934. Wanstead, Essex.

My dear Father,

It is with much pleasure that I inform you that I passed my examination at Addiscombe last Friday with credit, together with five others from here, and am a Gent. Cadet. I fear that the expenses of my education and dress for the last few years must have been severe, but I have hopes that for the short time I remain in England they will be slight compared with what they have been.

I feel that you and George have done everything in your power for me, so it remains for me to put a finishing stroke. Mr. Jones thinks I have some chance for Artillery, but I think I shall do very well if I get high in the Infantry, but this remains to be proved. You may depend on it I shall do all I can. About coming home, I think 10 days taking in Christmas Day and New Year's Day will be plenty as I should like to be a month here if possible; we are to be at Addiscombe the first Monday in February.

I dined with the Welches yesterday, I shall miss them when I get to Addiscombe. Capt. Macdonald came up with his son on Friday to be examined but he was plucked. I was at school with him at Radcliffes. I must not forget to thank you for the money which was very acceptable. George and Edward were both very well when I saw them on Tuesday. There is nothing new in town about the Ministry, the Duke is waiting for Sir R. Peel, and the Duke of Gloster is dying. Mr. Andrew desires to be remembered to you and says he shall have much pleasure in my company for the holidays. When you come to town you must run down to Addiscombe, it is a mile from Croydon in beautiful country.

Give my best love to all at Wylye, and mind always to write to me directing: – Wyndham Baker, Gentleman Cadet, and believe me to remain my dear Father,

Your affectionate Son,
Wyndham.

Let me hear soon your wishes respecting the holidays. Mr. Thornhill gave away three appointments including mine and I was the only one that passed. Frank gave me a long account of his proceedings the other day, he seems very content and happy.

Addiscombe.

October 31st, 1836.

My dear Father,

Within the last two months I have formed a great friendship for another cadet who goes out this term, i.e. gets his commission; his brothers are in the King's Service and one is in the Indian Civil Service. He and his Mother Mrs. Freese have determined to go to India. They think of sailing in the *Abercrombie Robinson*[1] on the 10th of January for Madras, and are anxious that I should accompany them.

The following are the advantages that I should gain by so doing. First, I should go out in one of the finest ships in the Navy. Secondly, I should have some pleasant companions during the voyage. Thirdly, it would be less expensive. Fourthly, I should on my arrival in India be with Mrs. Freese who has been out before and is acquainted with the Customs etc. besides which I shall have a capital introduction through the friends of her husband who was a Brigadier-General in the same Corps that I hope to be in – the Artillery.

The only thing I dislike about it is leaving you two months sooner than I am actually obliged to.

If you should fall in with anyone who may give me introductions to friends at Madras, don't scruple to ask them. The purport of this letter must not be lost sight of as most probably it will turn out of the greatest advantage to me. I am still obliged to work very hard. It often makes me very melancholy to think of what must take place within these two or three months at the latest, but this confounded weather is enough to make any of us melancholy.

Your affectionate Son,

Wyndham Baker.

1. *The* Abercrombie Robinson, *master Fraser, port of Registry London, built in London in 1725; 1425 tons. Wrecked Table Bay, August 28th, 1842. Later owned by East India Company.*

Addiscombe.
November 18th, 1836.

Mrs. F. Baker,
Wylye Rectory, Wilts.

My dear Mama,

As I have no doubt you are anxiously waiting to hear from me, I intend taking advantage of a spare half hour to inform you how my plans are at present. When I last wrote I had some fear about losing the Artillery, but with incessant hard studying I have left my competitors some way behind, indeed I think they intend now giving it up. But here's the rub, this prize that I have been looking forward to for so long a time and is now within my reach, turns out not worth having. Some of the Officers here have lately heard from some friends in the Artillery in India that the promotion in that Corps is so very slow that the Infantry is now the better service of the two. Of course this is very discouraging and I shall now leave it to chance. I wrote about a fortnight since to Mr. Thornhill asking him his advice about my accompanying Mrs. Freese to Madras. He wrote back to me that he would do all in his power at the India House to forward my wishes, and begged that I would come over there the following Saturday, the 12th. I found them kinder if anything than usual.

I have been making some enquiries at the outfitters about shirts etc. I find five dozen besides the ones I have by me are the very least I can take out, but as they are made of calico, they will be much cheaper than my others.

Mr. Welch tells me that he will give me an introduction to the Captain[1] of the *Abercrombie Robinson* which I am delighted to find does not sail before the 24th of January.

I shall write again in about a week's time and send you a short account of the ship. I must also trouble Papa for some money the next time he writes as it is beginning to be very scarce indeed here.

> With best love to him and Sisters.
> Your affectionate Son,
> Wyndham Baker.

This day three weeks I get my Commission. I only wish the public examination was over, the Duke of Wellington and many other grandees are expected down for it. I hope I shall not recognise any faces or I am certain to fail.

---

1. *Probably John Innes as he was Captain in 1832.*

Gordon Hotel,
Covent Garden.
Dec. 10th, 1836.

My dear Father,

It is with feelings of great pleasure I now address you. All my examinations have passed off very satisfactorily and I am now a 2nd Lieutenant in the Madras Artillery. I propose staying until Monday with the Welches to arrange my outfit etc. Monday night I shall go down to Mr. Lane's and start from there the following morning, after that my movements will be entirely directed by Julia's, but I hope to be with you at Wylye before the 21st. A party of 15 dined here yesterday and we are now just going to sit down to breakfast.

With my best love to Mama and Sisters.

Believe me to remain,
Your affectionate Son,
Wyndham Baker.

The Gordon Hotel,
Covent Garden
Jan. 28th, 1837.

My dear Father and Mother,

As I am now nearly settled with regard to my time of leaving this place. I think it right and proper to make you acquainted with everything I have done since my departure from Wylye. Of course my journey to town was anything but pleasant, but thank goodness I am in very good spirits now, and it is my earnest wish that you do not make yourself in the least uncomfortable about me, as I can assure you that no one can be better off than I am.

On entering my hotel, who should I see seated at one of the tables but George and Pyke, which of course eased my mind considerably. The next day, Tuesday, I introduced myself to the Freeses and I was engaged at Welche's in the City until dinner time, when I betook myself to Mrs. Hayes in the Temple (a particular friend of George's), where we dined and all went to the Italian opera in the evening.

Wednesday I was sworn in at the E.I. House (East India House) after which George drove me down to call on the Thornhills and we came back to a late dinner and the theatre in the evening. Yesterday I was in the City from 7 a.m. until 6 p.m. having packed everything up etc. I was delighted to find a letter waiting my arrival at Welche's from Papa and I paid for the cabin immediately, which by the by is changed and is now one of the best ones on the ship close to Mrs. F's.

The Davises have been kind enough to send me some nice books and George has presented me with some capital standard works which will be of the greatest service. I go down to the Thornhills to-day and shall return to-morrow. Mrs. T. has the watch awaiting my arrival and young T. tells me it is a very nice one. Mr. T. seemed very much pleased with your attention in writing to him, but he did not mention the dressing-case so I shall have to get one myself.

I shall go down with the F.s to Portsmouth on Monday or Tuesday, so I fear there is no possibility of our meeting again for some time; the ship sails on Wednesday and the wind is just in the proper place. Welche has got me some nice plate and I consider he has fitted me out capitally. I am fearful from what Mamma says in Mrs. F.'s letter that she is suffering a good deal from influenza still, but I hope it will go off directly.

No one can imagine what a hurry and confusion I have been in ever since I came up, indeed had I stayed with you till Tuesday I should never have had my things ready in time for the ship.

Hoping that you are much better and that my next epistle will find you in perfect health.

Believe me to remain,
Your most affectionate Son,
Wyndham.

(Note on this letter written by his mother. "Leave taken of us the Monday before, on the 23rd. of January – that was a melancholy day.")

(Written on the back of this letter.) 5 a.m. no bed yet,
Friday morning.

My dear Sisters,

I cannot allow this portmanteau to leave without enclosing a short letter to you. The chain[1] has been universally admired and I think it the neatest I ever beheld, mind to send it back thro' the Davises immediately to Mr. Welche's, you can't think how much I value it.

No nightgown of J.B.'s in my trunk.

George leaves this morning.

I have tried at 20 places to get a tambour needle[2] for Louisa but all in vain. You shall hear from me again very soon and believe me, with best love to all at Wylye.

Your most affectionate brother,
Wyndham Baker.

134 Leadenhall Street,
Wednesday morning,
Feb. 1st, 1837.

My dear Father,

As I find Mr. Davies is going down to-day I cannot lose the opportunity of just informing you how I am at present situated. To-morrow morning I go down to Portsmouth with George, and the rest of the party will come down the same day by another conveyance; we shall most likely embark the same afternoon. I have received your nice letters and I am delighted to find you are all well again.

Mrs. Thornhill has given me a beautiful little watch (15 guineas' worth), but as Mr. T. forgot the dressing-case I have purchased one myself. Mr. T. desired me to say he was obliged to you for your kind letters and was sorry you did not accompany me up here. I have received some nice books from the Davis' such as Cowper's "Friendships and Remembrances" etc. I have

---

1. *This was a chain made of strands of hair from the heads of all his sisters, which were then eight in number.*
2. *A tambour was a small hollow drum or frame on which muslin or other material was stretched for embroidery.*

purchased a capital gun for £15. 10s. I consider I have a most capital outfit and have been very well treated at Welche's, and shall write to you again directly the Pilot leaves the ship; and will, if sickness does not prevent me, be more profuse in my writing.

I am in capital spirits and therefore hope you will not make yourselves at all miserable about a person who considers himself very well off. Tell Louisa I have purchased a tambour needle for her, but am sorry it is of an inferior kind to the pattern, however it is the best I could get. I had intended having my picture taken but I could not as my time would not allow it. I wished to have sent my sisters some little keepsakes but I think I had better put it off until I get to India. Now, my dear Father, I must with you every happiness this world can afford, and I trust that when we meet again you will find that I have proved myself worthy of that kindness which you and my family have ever bestowed upon me; and hoping we shall all see better days and with best love to my Mother and every branch of my family particularly my dear Sisters.

Believe me ever to remain,
Your most affectionate son,
Wyndham Baker.

(The last letter received from England) The George Hotel,
Portsmouth.
Feb. 4th, 1837.

The Rev. F. Baker,
Wylye Rectory,
Wilts.

My dear Father,

In half an hour I embark in the *Abercrombie Robinson*, she lies about six miles from hence on the motherbank. I find I have everything required on board and dare say I shall soon get settled. I intend, if I possibly can, to give you a line when the Pilot leaves us, as I have no doubt you are very anxious to know something about me. Pray when you write to remember to send the letters thro' Mr. Thornhill and they will then find me sooner than if you sent them per pool.

I wish one of you would be kind enough to write to my brother George and tell him I should have written only I have hardly had one moment I can call my own. And now my dear Father let me bid you and all my beloved relations a long adieu and should fate prevent our again meeting here, it is my earnest hope that we may all once again meet where nothing can separate us from each other. Tell my sisters that although seas will separate us, I shall never cease to think of them, and with best love to my poor Mother, Eliza, Frank and all my dear family.

Believe me to remain and be,
Your affectionate son,
Wyndham Baker.

We have a fair wind and by the time this reaches you I shall be out of sight of dear England.

On board the good ship
Abercrombie Robinson,
Saturday night Feb. 4th, 1837.

The Rev. F. Baker,
Wylye Rectory,
Wilts

My dear Father,

As the pilot leaves us in a few minutes, I take the opportunity of his going on shore of writing you a few lines. We have passed the Needles about an hour [ago]. It blows pretty hard and there is a tremendous swell and I feel very sick, all the ladies are unwell and so are some of the gents, but I suppose we shall soon get used to it. We only came on board about five o'clock and to-morrow morning we shall be out of sight of land.

I am so very poorly I must wish you goodbye for the present and with best love to all.

Believe me to remain,
Yours,
Wyndham.

(This letter was covered in blots. Poor Wyndham was evidently feeling very "mal de mer." –
Editor.)

In the *Abercrombie Robinson*,
Monday night, Feb. 13th, 1837.

My dear Father,

Immediately on going on board, our ship fired a salute of 15 guns as we weighed anchor, in honour of Sir Willoughby Cotton, who had arrived only a few minutes before us. The wind being exactly in our favour we soon ran through the Needles and in the course of the night stood some way out to sea. From Saturday night to Thursday I was so unwell that I kept my bed all the time and indeed so was nearly every person in the ship. Thursday, Friday and Saturday nights we had the most dreadful storms which came on every night as the sun went down, – you can imagine nothing half so awful as a storm at sea.

The whole week we were beating about in Latitude 48° 25', Longitude 13° 15', losing one day what we had gained the previous. On Sunday the storm commenced about night as usual and about 12 o'clock we sprang a leak so the men were obliged to be at the pumps night and day, besides which a great number of the seamen were so laid up that the Captain determined on putting into port and this morning we found ourselves in a direct course for Falmouth. I had hoped to see you at Wylye but the Captain says he will not stay more than 48 hours.

Perhaps you would like to know some of our arrangements on board: we get up to breakfast at nine, which is generally a very excellent one, plenty of good meat etc.; we have luncheon at 12, it consists merely of a little wine and biscuits; dinner at three and a capital one it is, two or three joints of mutton, poultry, soups, puddings etc., besides salt meats. After dinner the ladies leave us and we take our wine very comfortably for an hour or so; we tea at eight and go to bed at about half past ten; the only disagreeable part on board ship is the continual rolling and the want of fresh water, we are only allowed a pint of fresh water a day for washing, which you know is hardly enough.

9 p.m. I have just arrived at the Royal Hotel, Falmouth, if the wind should change to S.E. or S.W. we shall leave immediately, at any rate let me hear from you directly on receipt of this letter.

With my best love to Mother and all sisters and brothers.

Believe me to remain,
Your affectionate son,
Wyndham Baker.

Pearces Royal Hotel,
Falmouth,
Feb: 22nd, 1837.

The Rev. Frances Baker,
Wylye Rectory,
Wilts.

My dear Father,

I fear on the receipt of this letter you will be rather displeased at not having heard from me before to acknowledge the letter and money which has proved very acceptable, but the truth is that I have been so harassed with contrary reports concerning the wind and sailing of the ship, that I determined on putting off writing to you until I could actually state the day I shall leave this place. I have now been staying here at little more than a week and I think I can safely state that during that time the wind has changed every half hour, so my time has been chiefly taken up in going to and from the ship. Of course, had I been able to have looked into futurity, I should have taken the earliest opportunity of putting myself on the Devonport Mail, and spending the last week with you, where I would prefer spending it to any place on earth.

I have to thank you or rather my Mother for her kindness in copying Edward's letter which amused as well as gratified me exceedingly. It seems that we are both destined to go through a good deal both on land and water. I have to inform you that I shall ever consider it a divine interposition of providence that I am now in existence as the ship when we entered this harbour was in a most shattered condition, and had we been out one more day nothing could have prevented our going down. Every day since our arrival there have been fresh ships coming in, some dismasted, others complete wrecks; indeed an Indiaman of our own tonnage, which sailed only a few days after us, has been picked up by a packet going out. She was found without a soul on board, and I dare say you will see something of it in the papers – but enough of this gloomy subject, we sail for certain this day and I have very little doubt we shall have better luck. If I should happen to fall in with any ship you may depend upon it I will let you hear from me. I have heard from Parnell and I will give him a letter if I possibly can. If I don't you will let him know the reason why. Harriett (who by the way was the only one of my sisters to give me a line) wished to know if Chester the passenger was a Devon man. His name was Bagut, a Bucks. family and he was a pupil of the Dean's. Mrs. F. desires her compliments to all our family.

I am sorry to say the sailors are very discontented on board our ship, and the ship is likely to see a little disturbance before we arrive at Madras.

However all male passengers are armed with pistols and swords so I can't conceive there can be any damage done.

And now I again wish you goodbye, and with kindest regards and remembrances to all at home.

Believe me to remain,

Your affectionate son,

Wyndham Baker.

On board the *Abercrombie Robinson*,
Monday, March 20th, 1837.

The Rev. Frances Baker,
Wylye Rectory,
Wiltshire.

My dear Father,

We sailed from Falmouth on Saturday the 25th, and up to this day have had an uninterrupted series of fair and fine weather, and have made upwards of 3,000 miles in 23 days, which is an average of 130 miles a day. We were at Falmouth 11 days and on leaving the harbour came in contact with one of the King's ships and almost knocked her to pieces but suffered very little ourselves; this has been our only mishap as yet. On the 1st we crossed the Bay of Biscay safely and on the 4th were within 100 miles of Madeira but could not see the Island. We here fell in with a ship about four miles off and hailed her, but she did not answer our signals and showed the Pirates' Colours, so we soon put up all sail and got out of her way. The following is our mode of speaking at sea: we have 10 different flags which are recognised 1, 2, 3 and 4 etc., our ship's number is 6293, so we put up the flags answering to those numbers by referring to the key; any other is able to find out directly. In this manner we can converse on almost any subject at a great distance off.

On the 7th we passed through the Canaries and this was the first very warm day. I witnessed this day for the first time a burial at sea. The ceremony is nearly the same as it is on land but is better conducted at sea I think, the men are more attentive and show more respect than any congregation that I have been used to. On the 12th we passed close to the Cape Verde Islands and to-day have just crossed the Line. You have all heard I dare say of the ceremony of shaving on crossing the Line; we have all just gone through that operation, and altho' we all had to pay £1, yet they did not let us off without a great many bruises and plenty of tar. It is quite impossible for you to conceive how hot it is and I am in a continual fever. If it is as hot as this in India it is impossible for me to exist, the skin peels off my hands and feet and I feel too lazy to move.

The time passes agreeably enough on board and I get on very comfortably but you can hardly imagine the little petty rows that are going on which always originate with the ladies. I have not yet fallen in love nor do I ever intend to now, as I fear I should be obliged to go over the whole world before I am suited.

There is a very pleasant fellow on board of the name of Dalrymple and we amuse ourselves fishing for sharks etc. all the morning, and on Sunday caught one nearly 14 feet long – a very different sport from fishing at Wylye as I require two or three men to hold the line, and it's rather more dangerous as when we get the fish on board he strikes all around him with his tail and the other day a man was killed by a blow. We see a great many dolphins, porpoises and flying fish.

I was very much afraid when we left Falmouth that we should have a Mutiny before the end of the voyage, but we are all right again now and I fancy we shall get to Madras in the course of two months or so, that is if everything goes on prosperously.

I do not think there is any chance of our falling in with another ship till the end of the voyage, so you must not expect to hear from me for another four months after you receive this. Captain Cotton, Sir W.'s son has been staying at the Davises, he is the most complete blackguard and I have given up his acquaintance.

With my very best love to all at home, likewise at Bathford, Peterstown, Hereford and Tellisford.

Believe me to remain,
Your most affectionate son,
Wyndham Baker.

Madras

Wyndham Baker arrived in the *Abercrombie Robinson* on Saturday May 27th, 1837. His voyage had taken only 13 weeks from Falmouth but, as we have made clear from his letters, he had embarked on 4th February, so had spent three weeks in the Channel before finally starting from Falmouth on the 25th.

By a queer chance we already possess the published diary of Lieut. J.S. Cumming of the 9th Foot who arrived in Madras Roads in the very same weekend though on a different vessel. By the standard of those days the voyage was a fairly rapid one, which we may compare with the six and a half months it took Philip Francis to reach Calcutta in 1774 and one of the voyages of 19 weeks described in the same decade which are recounted in "Ladies in the Sun."

The passengers on the *Abercrombie Robinson* had clearly had a bad time from the weather and there had been a lot of what Baker calls in various letters "disputes" and "little petty rows which always originate with the ladies." It is also clear that the sailors "were very discontented on board" a fact which led Lieutenant Cumming to remark "There is not a seaman on board who does not detest the sea."

Nor were the hazards of the voyage completely over on arrival in Madras Roads. It was a very bad anchorage with heavy surf alongshore and there was no proper harbour at that time equipped with a deep water quay. This was only completed 90 or more years later. Shoal water stretched seawards for two miles. Henry Dodwell has described how the landing of passengers was accomplished "in *masula* boats, built of yielding *anjali* planks sewn together. Into one of these you would jump at the peril of a soaking and be rowed ashore... and after passing through the surf with your heart in your mouth you would be carried to dry land on the back of a wet and slippery fisherman." According to Kincaid, this task was often undertaken by chivalrous subalterns "from the garrison who always hurried on board... to see if there were any ladies disembarking" – an odd method of introduction which must be left to the imagination.

Wyndham Baker's first letter notes that "Mrs. Freese" (a lady for whom, though a family acquaintance, he had obviously conceived a lively detestation as "the very essence of all deceit and falsehood") went ashore on the Saturday evening they arrived, as did most of the other passengers but they made a bad landing.

"The surf was so high and rough that two boats were upset only a few minutes before they got on shore. I stayed on board that night intending to land next day, but the Captain would not allow any boat to go on shore till Tuesday. On Saturday there were five Europeans and three natives drowned and Mrs. Freese's boat was as nearly swamped as possible" – a remark in which we can trace some sardonic pleasure.

At exactly the same time John Cumming was writing "We are now snugly anchored off Madras Roads though there is a fearful surf on the beach... Indeed on Sunday two gentlemen lost their lives and one lady was much injured", so Baker's delay in disembarking can be understood and in a later letter he mentioned three ships being driven ashore in one night of October.

Baker's letter, written from the Barracks on St. Thomas's Mount some miles out of Madras goes on:

"Immediately on landing I was obliged to report myself to the Fort where I was most agreeably surprised to find many old Addiscombe friends. On Wednesday I received orders to report my arrival to a Capt. Polwhell, the Adjutant General, who without any introduction insisted on my taking up my abode with him until I could fix on a bungalow."

Ultimately Baker moved to St. Thomas's Mount. These barracks must have been of comparatively recent origin. In 1791 William Hickey had noted how Tippoo's freebooters had come close to Madras and "likewise burnt or wantonly destroyed most of the European gentlemen's country seats at the Mount, Choultry Plain and the neighbourhood in every direction of Fort St. George" as well as the huge and expensive cavalry barracks at Wallaujaubad.

Since then, Madras City had grown exceedingly in size and population, though Cumming thought little of it: "Madras has quite disappointed my expectations. There are only one or two good houses in the place; the rest are small shabby houses, inhabited by poor people". Baker, writing to his sister Isabella a few months later, is less restrained.

"The approach to Madras from the sea," he says in a letter dated 13th April, 1838, "is striking in the extreme. The beach almost appears alive with the crowds that cover it. Most of the houses by the sea are supported on colonnades and they are stuccoed with such a beautiful kind of mortar that it looks like marble, being very white, hard, smooth and polished. The country immediately around Madras has a barren and flat appearance, and every here and there you see a hill rising up some 400 or 500 feet, about as suddenly as the tumuli on Salisbury Plain. St. Thomas' Mount is one of these. Fort St. George is close to the sea, its walls and bastions present an interesting appearance, at a distance you see minarets, churches and pagodas mixed with the trees."

A fortnight after his arrival Baker had moved out of Madras itself and in a letter dated 11th June he describes to his father his life as a supernumerary officer of the Madras Artillery and the queer routine, superimposed by the European's universal fear of the climate, in which all military work ceased a few hours after dawn, much as Sir Winston Churchill described it 50 years later as a subaltern in the 4th Hussars.

"The heat here in the middle of the day is perfectly unbearable. Indeed no-one thinks of leaving the house until 6 o'clock in the evening. Every person rises at 5 (the Barrack guns fire), I am obliged to drill from 5 to 6 and ride afterwards till half past seven: then we come in to take a cup of coffee and go to sleep for an hour, then bathe and breakfast about 9. At 10 my Hindoo tutor comes and I study with him for two hours and employ myself as most convenient until the dinner or tiffin hour. We either take this meal at our houses or go to the Mess at the Barracks. People generally take a nap from five to six and ride out afterwards, after six it is delightful out-of-doors as the sun sets at seven and there is no twilight. This is the fashionable hour for ladies to go out driving, and as the Mount Road is the fashionable drive we see nearly everybody up here. At seven we sup at the Mess House and usually sit down 18 or 20. People here drink very little wine, beer is the favourite beverage and most delicious it is, superior to any I tasted in England. If we do not go to sup at the Mess we call in at any private house and there are some always bidding a welcome, indeed I do not see any of that formality which is so common in England. After a little music or dancing the party breaks up and we retire to our rooms at 11 o'clock – and thus the day is spent in India."

It will be seen from this account that the prolonged all-male carouses, "pushing the claret about freely", which William Hickey described so often in Calcutta, were by 1837 not so common in Madras, a land already with enormous European graveyards and a bad record for sickness of every kind. Presumably, from Calcutta catalogues we possess, the beer drunk was Bass or Allsops pale ales imported in hogsheads, and not a local brew.

Living was very cheap. As a subaltern Baker received Rs.200 a month or £20 and could "live comfortably" on about Rs. 165, which included "Mess 70 rupees, house rent 15 or 20, subscriptions to military library and Club house 40 and servants 35 rupees". We may note that this last sum, equivalent to £3.10/- a month, was sufficient to pay no less than eight servants: a butler, a valet or dressing-boy, "a waterman who does nothing but keep my bath full, washer-woman, a tailor and shoemaker, one horse keeper, and one grass cutter for the horse; so I am become quite a man of authority as a person cannot live here without quite a number of servants as the heat makes one weak and languid; but the thing I dread most is the cholera and the jungle fever which is very prevalent here now. Since I landed I have heard of no less then three of my old companions, who died the second month after they arrived here."

Dodwell, who made a careful study of the Madras records for the 50 years ending 1800, noted that 50 per cent of the men coming out in those years were dead within five years of arrival, quite apart from casualties in war. There were no hill stations, and medical science was still very much in its infancy. The fact that cholera was waterborne and that the mosquito was the carrier of malaria had not yet been established, nor apparently had the use of teak in building, as Baker complains bitterly of the ravages of white ants in his bungalow.

A further letter (25th August, 1837) shows him acclimatised: "I am now quite settled and as happy as I can possibly expect to be in India.

Indeed I have no cause whatever for complaint as I have been very kindly received here, and as far as the climate goes, I never was better in my life except that the heat makes me very weak... We never dare take any exercise in the middle of the day; some go out shooting but it is very dangerous. I generally ride out in the mornings from five till seven and either hunt jackals or hyenas in the afternoon or play at cricket: the latter is much played here and is a very favourite amusement."

Social events clearly filled an inordinate a part in the life of the European as they did a century later and the same intolerance (which Emily Eden was to observe acidly a few months later) towards even the princes of India (whose ancestry could probably be traced as far or even further back than that of most Europeans) is well exemplified in the same letter.

"I went to a grand ball at the Governor's a little while ago. The whole turn-out was on a most liberal and magnificent scale, the *élite* of Madras would not go as Lord and Lady Brudenell[1] were invited." "It is quite an uncommon thing to see a gentleman in a black coat at a Ball, as nearly every person is in uniform which makes the room look very well.

"The Governor always invites the Nabob to his parties and it is the most ridiculous thing to see a handsome young man like Lord Elphinstone walking arm-in-arm with these black people and he is obliged to kiss them all when they come and go." [We may suspect that this custom of kissing was one which had survived the French occupation and capture of Madras in 1745 by Dupleix: it had certainly died out in the late Victorian era.] "The Nabob was formerly in possession of a greater part of India with a revenue of four or five millions, but when the East India Company took this country they kindly pensioned him with about 100,000 a year with which he is very well-satisfied and keeps up a pretty court."

He goes on to describe how this Nawab (obviously a Musulman) came up for worship at a mosque and offered an Arabian horse to each of the three British officers on his guard of honour, a

---

1. *Lord Brudenell was held responsible by relatives of the gallant dead after the Charge of the Light Brigade. (See* The Reason Why *by Cecil Woodham Smith).*

"gratification", in the words of the Government Servants' Conduct Rules, which they all had to refuse on pain of being cashiered.

Times had indeed changed by 1837 since the days when men came out to India, with all its lethal risks, hoping to make their fortunes from such gifts or bribes; since the days of Clive who left India with a fortune of about a million sterling and a known income of £45,000; since William Hickey's friend Bob Pott had the Nawab of Bengal's stipend through his hands "in which channel a considerable portion of it always stuck to his fingers"; since the Residency at Benares was worth £30,000 a year in bribes to the son of Archbishop Markham.

Now Baker laments that "the Government found formerly that there was a great deal of bribing carried on in this manner and were obliged to put a stop to it, so we are the sufferers, now obliged to depend on prize money in war.

His letters home concentrate on his social engagements and there is hardly a hint of work. "Talking of Balls, we are just going to give a grand one to all the people of Madras and neighbourhood . . . the people tell me they are the best Balls in India, indeed they ought to be very good considering the splendid band" (the Madras Artillery maintained a European band of 30 instruments) "and rooms we have. I only wish I could present my sisters at them to show everyone how to dance."

This letter adds that "the cholera is raging in a most terrible degree up country... A detachment of 113th Cavalry were coming down the other day and they lost 74 men on the road and in the same regiment eight officers have died within little more than two months." Fifty years later one of Kipling's officers was to notice how the British cavalry "took to cholera."

The native population normally form a dusky and unregarded background to the life of Europeans in India, but there is one vivid glimpse of them in this letter. "I witnessed a most extraordinary sight the other day. The natives once a year, if they have done anything very wicked during the preceding year, do penance by allowing themselves to have a hook put under their ribs and are suspended in this manner for some minutes, 50 feet high. There can be no description as they are quite naked and the wound is disgusting. I only mentioned this to show what idiots we have to deal with." He adds a passing reference to the practice of *suttee* – "this *favour* is not allowed by the Government now", though Emily Eden later laments that "two of those poor dear ranees whom we visited, and thought so beautiful and so merry, have actually burnt themselves," so it was a law occasionally disregarded even in Baker's day.

In this letter dated 25th August 1837 (just after the accession of Queen Victoria) there are two points which deserve mention. Baker had written previously that wine was seldom drunk in the Cantonment and everyone drank "delicious" beer. He now writes, "The same beer in England would be considered bitter and unpalatable but the voyage makes it quite a different thing. We drink beer with each other at dinner with all the formalities of drinking wine."

We already know that the wine of Madeira was considered to be vastly improved by the rolling it got from going once or even twice round the Cape in the hold of a ship, so much so that gentlemen in Madras had their imported pipes of Madeira "spun" in their own cellars, a practice which was locally known as "giving them a voyage round the Cape". We know also that 11 years after Baker's arrival, hogsheads of pale English ale from this country were being auctioned in Calcutta. Presumably it was these hogsheads which were improved by the rolling of a long voyage.

We have one other intriguing glimpse of Baker's life in Madras. Writing to his father in the peace of the Wylye valley he says, "I think you would not like the mode of driving about in this country. For instance, a gentleman never drives without two men at the very least running by the side to keep the flies off the horse. I never ride out without the horse keeper following me; it is quite wonderful how these fellows run and never complain."

When this tyrannical custom died, as die it did, we do not know but in an earlier letter (dated 11th June 1837) he says of the much-enduring Madrassi that "the men here will run five miles an hour with a Palanquin and keep it up for hours. I can send a large box on a man's back for 15 miles and he will be satisfied with sixpence," about four annas, a sum which can only be described as the reward of sweated labour.

William IV had died on 13th June. Was Baker's letter wishing his father "once more adieu as the ship sails almost immediately, with my kindest love to Mother, sisters and brothers," one of the earliest received in the Victorian era of which we know? The cheapness of provisions does not escape him. "I can get a fine ox for 15 rupees or 30 shillings, fowls 6d. a couple and so on; the sheep are much smaller than the English but I like them just as much, better flavoured I think. At a dinner you sometimes see four or five different sorts of curry, some of them most excellent, nothing like our English curries, not so hot. All wines are cheaper than in England except port which is very seldom drunk."

In a letter dated 1st November also to his father, he says "The rainy season has just set in, and it is like September or May in England as regards the heat but there is much more rain. This weather continues till about the middle of March I believe, when most likely I shall leave this for up country . . . People began to dread a failure in the crops which would almost create a famine amongst the natives and the cholera was raging dreadfully, but directly the rain set in all our gloomy fears vanished and everything wears a brighter aspect."

It is also clear that the Madras Presidency took its hot weathers much more seriously than other parts of India. "People in this country pay no attention to out-of-door amusements; gardening is out of the question. Indeed ladies seem to consider it a great exertion to ride in a carriage and listen to a Band, a Ball knocks them up for days, so this would never suit my sisters who are so fond of walking in the open air. I still keep up my fame in the waltzing department . . . One of the most acceptable presents you could send me would be some common tortoise-shell eye-glasses, numbers four and five, as they are most expensive out here and my eyes are getting worse I fear . . . At Bangalore where the climate is nearly approaching to England" [and to which he was hoping to be posted] "they have peaches and all kinds of English fruits and vegetables. I have just begun to wear cloth trousers, having worn nothing but linen since I left England except round the Cape . . . which will give you some idea of the hot season we have here."

In a letter, already partly-quoted, to his sister Isabella dated 13th April 1838, he writes: "About four miles from Madras stands a Cenotaph to the memory of Lord Cornwallis" (the able Governor who stopped the rot in 1807 when Tippoo Sahib was at the zenith of his career, as William Hickey noted) "and we are about to erect another to Sir Thomas Munro". "The statue itself is by Chantrey" (who had recently become Sir Frances and was probably the most noted sculptor of his age) "and is expected out by one of the next ships and it is supposed that the expense of getting it across the surf will be more than the other expenses put together."

The letter goes on: "It is customary for the ladies and gents. to repair in the gayest equipage to the Mount Road in the cool of the evening where they drive slowly round this Cenotaph conversing together and detailing all the news and scandal they can get hold of. The Governor has been very gay lately, about a month since Prince Henry of Holland, one of the sons of the Prince of Orange, spent a month here at the Governor's House. During his stay we sent him an invitation to a Ball at our Mess House, but he was engaged for every day and had not a moment to call his own, however he came up for a review we had for him, and expressed himself highly gratified at our manoeuvres. He is only about 20 years old and brought up for the Navy, they say he is remarkably like me, however that is not very complimentary as he is undoubtedly the plainest man I ever saw.

"Lord and Lady Cardigan have also been staying with the Governor on their route from Calcutta home, and now Sir F. Maitland, and Admiral, with all his staff, and wife, with some other ladies are there. I have been to a great number of parties there lately and waltz as much as ever. There is a report just arrived that the Governor is to be sent home immediately, they say also that the young Queen is very fond of him and is going to make proposals to him . . .

"I have just returned from church, the Governor was there with a very large party, he always goes about with four horses to his carriage and an escort of soldiers and is quite a king out here. I have just heard that an express has been received this morning from Calcutta, ordering over two Regiments to Rangoon or rather Moulmein, so it appears we have still some chance of a war in that quarter... I believe though that it will all end in smoke as they only send over these men just to show we are prepared for a rupture." Cumming of the 9th Foot had several months earlier been anticipating that his regiment would move from Chinsura to Moulmein in Burma: "Should we go there we should be under the necessity of building houses for our accommodation which would be very expensive and Government do not allow any compensation."

But this move never came off, and the next we hear is in September 1838 when Baker, still only a supernumerary but with his pay raised to £260 and in command of a Company, was transferred to Secunderabad. Indian troops had no pensions to which to look forward in those days but "we are about to establish a Retiring Fund which will facilitate promotion". Even up to 1920 the Indian Civil Service suffered a four per cent deduction from their pay which went towards their pension funds and they were the most privileged of the Indian services.

Secunderabad

From a letter written a few months after his arrival, it was obvious that Wyndham Baker had hoped to be posted to Bangalore, a Cantonment in the state of Mysore about 150 miles due west of Madras, which was probably then used as a hot-weather station. "It is a beautiful climate much more like Italy than any other I believe."

However, in July 1838 he was suddenly ordered off with a detachment 400 miles north to Secunderabad. It was a testing assignment for a young officer as he had only one English NCO and was in charge of a hundred natives besides some cannon. The rivers were unbridged and the Krishna River "which is very deep and rapid occupied me three days in crossing as I was obliged to take all the gun-carriages to pieces to get them into the little wicker boats which took me across."

The letter gives a vivid glimpse of the routine of a hot weather march. "We used to strike our tents at 1 a.m. precisely and march at 2 every day and I seldom ever got to the encamping grounds before 10 o'clock, the distance generally about 12 miles, so we went just about one mile and a half an hour. At 10 o'clock the sun was of course very high and the heat passing through the jungles overpowering. You can imagine how refreshing a bottle of water is in such cases, with which I used to indulge myself instead of breakfast and forget all my troubles in a sound sleep for a few hours." It is clear that the ubiquitous tea, with or without tinned milk, which sustained so many generations of his successors in hot climates was unknown, though "green and black tea" were then served on ship and Mrs. Fay, whose last letter from India was dated 1815, drank tea every afternoon "as a drug that cleanses the stomach and digests the superfluous humours".

After waking, the young officer would "saunter out for a few hours with my gun on my shoulder and perhaps if I had any luck bring back some game after an hour's shooting which would be cooked and on the table for dinner at 6 o'clock, which over a cigar and a glass of brandy and water would occupy me till 8, when I went to bed."

This routine, comprising the start in the dark, the comparatively short march of 10 or 12 miles, the midday sleep, the afternoon *shikar*, and the infinitely leisurely journey, was familiar to all touring officers in India, for the next century. Baker reached Secunderabad in six weeks, on 31st August, and "during that time I only saw four white faces besides the afore mentioned Sergeant. Although cholera was prevalent I did not lose a man which was a rare occurrence at this season on a long march . . ."

"You can hardly imagine what an immense Cantonment this is. There is one Queen's Regiment, six companies of Infantry and one Regiment of Cavalry, besides Horse and Foot Artillery, so when we are all mustered on Parade I can assure you it is a sight well worth seeing. Within five miles of this there is another large force belonging to the Nizam and in the other direction is the renowned city of Hyderabad where the Nizam resides and keeps up a splendid court with Eastern magnificence."

On one occasion Baker obtained "a ticket" allowing him to accompany the English Resident, Colonel Fraser, on a formal visit to the Nizam. "We were obliged to go on elephants, of which there were at least 50 employed for the occasion. The Palace is very fine but the men (all Mussulmen) were the finest I ever saw. The dinner, at which the natives came to look at us but of which they did not partake, was the very best I ever saw on table, champagne in abundance, fruits the finest that India can produce etc. After the entertainment was over there was a grand display of fireworks and baskets filled with little bottles of Oil of Roses were handed round as presents. I pocketed 10 little bottles each worth at least 10/-, so the Nizam did not make much by me but the servants pilfer them if the Europeans don't take them." [Gone were the days when Wyndham Baker was terrified of being cashiered for accepting a gift from a native!] "At 10 o'clock the Resident rose and kissed the Nizam and we went back as we came."

Again we may note the incessant social round of the European. "We are exceedingly gay people at this station; hardly a night passes without a Ball or play or some fun or other. I have not been out much as yet, as of course in such a large society it takes some time to become acquainted with people. A band plays here every evening and you would be astonished at the number of people who attend it, some 20 ladies on horseback attended by twice as many gentlemen, besides carriages, phaetons, gigs etc. innumerable."

"We hear of nothing but War on every side and doubtless it will sooner or later come to a crisis. The papers state that we have declared War with the people of Cabul [Afghanistan] and Nepal and there must be some foundation for the report as expresses have been sent to order Regiments up into part immediately; indeed Bangalore, where there is nearly as large a Force as there is here, is now wholly without Troops. Persia and Burmah look inclined to be pugnacious also."

His hopes of proceeding on active service were faint, however, as the Indian Government was obliged by treaty to maintain certain numbers of troops in the Nizam of Hyderabad's dominions.

The unabashed nepotism of that time (which Kipling noted later, and on which the young Winston Churchill counted on freely to get a chance of active service in the 'nineties) is well exemplified in two extracts from Wyndham Baker's home letters. "Report says that the Governor, Lord Elphinstone, has received an order to return home immediately, if so I hope you [his sister Georgina] will manage to get me introduced to the new Governor." Later in a letter dated 26th November to his mother, he says "Let me beg of you not to miss an opportunity of getting me introductions to people high in office as Lord Auckland [the Governor-General of India) or Sir Jasper Nicolls [Commander-in-Chief] as it might make my future. There are some vacancies in our Horse Artillery which is the finest in the world and it would be the summit of my ambition to fill one of these."

A year later the all-observant Emily Eden at Delhi rode with her brother through "an immense crowd for besides all the regiments here people have come from all parts just to ask for what they can get; appointments are filled up in November because all the sick people . . . get their furloughs for going home. G. [George Eden, Lord Auckland] hates Delhi from the very circumstance of all these applicants."

The latter months of 1838 were full of troop movements and rumours of war. "We are still very full of War," Baker writes on 26th November, "but I do not think it will come to much on this side of

India. Rangoon is our only chance but it is supposed the Bengal and Bombay armies will have plenty of it before long. They are now on their route to Herat which is besieged by the Persians and will probably fall before we can assist our allies. Calcutta is 1800 miles from Kabul which will probably be the seat of this war, so you can imagine what a time will expire before we know how things will end.

"The Bombay Force have embarked and will go by water as far as they can by Indus river and the Bengal Force have only their legs to trust to for that immense distance."

So short of troops was the Bombay Presidency as a result of these moves, that just before Christmas Baker was ordered to "put my Company of Artillery in readiness to march immediately to Ahmednagar, a station in the Bombay Presidency 140 miles from Bombay which is to be occupied by Madras Troops in consequence of all the Bombay People having left for Sind. Of course this disconcerted me much as I was obliged to send all my furniture and provide myself with marching equipage. I had just put myself into proper train when an officer came up to supersede me..." which meant for him some financial loss and the need to re-purchase his old belongings "at double the price they fetched. But we are rough and ready chaps and as soldiers must obey. I think this sort of life would stagger one of your swell Regent Street Hussars who are made for nothing but show." What regiment was thus designated we alas do not know, but 102 years later similar phrases such as "Groppi's Light Horse", and "the Gaberdine Swine" could be heard in Cairo to describe those smartly-dressed soldiers who did not like the Western Desert.

A letter in May 1839 says: "The armies of Bombay and Bengal are getting on very well on their route to Candahar; no obstacles have yet offered themselves. The high price of beer, wine, and cheroots seems to harass them more than anything else." Emily Eden's acidulous pen noted, in November of that year, of returning officers that "all deny the report of the army having suffered further distress than a want of wine and cigars and they are all looking uncommonly fat." In fact, one cavalry regiment brought back a pack of foxhounds which it had taken on the expedition.'

Few young officers in the East ever escaped getting into debt, a fact which Kipling noted many years later. In April 1839, nearly two years after his arrival, Baker wrote to his father to say "I have been in debt but am now well out of the scrape, remitting £10 to £15 monthly to my creditors." (As his pay in India had started at £20 a month and had now risen by only about £20 a year i.e. to £260, this appears a heavy burden, but I think it possible that for £10 we should read Rs. 10.) He adds: "Do not attribute this to extravagance, gambling or any cause of that sort. The whole was occasioned by my being stationed so long near the Residency and being a member of that splendid mess of ours at the Mount and my having too many young friends." A later letter adds that to live comfortably on his pay and save 10 or 15 rupees a month as he was doing, is not bad "as I don't think there are 10 men in 100 in this country who live within the limits of their pay."

He also for once expands the meagre details he had so far given about the Madras Artillery. "My Corps is comprised of six Regiments, two of those Artillery and four of Foot and each Regiment is divided into four Companies or Troops; three out of the four Regiments of Foot are entirely Europeans, the fourth Natives. I am at present [N.B. as a 2nd Lieutenant] in charge of a European Company, for which I get the small sum of 30 Rupees or £3 a month and have an infinity of trouble besides the responsibility of about 6,000 Rupees going through my hands monthly. For this paltry sum I have to take care of 110 Europeans, see to their accounts and am answerable for their messing etc. Europeans in this country are so very careless of themselves that they require looking after just like schoolboys. To each Company there are also about 100 Natives attached, 30 as Lascars and 70 as drivers, so that the Company consists of upwards of 200 men altogether. I have the honour of commanding six 9-Pounders on parade, which combined with the *esprit de corps* which all Artillery men possess to a certain extent, in part repays me for my trouble… I anticipate being a Lieutenant in the course of a year or two. Our Retiring Fund is rather severe on the young hands but as we shall ultimately be the gainers by it, we have little cause to complain."

There is a little gossip in these letters of, for example, a serious outbreak of cholera at Bellary and "a sad disturbance" really a minor mutiny, led by the ship's officers, mate, mid-shipmen and "younger passengers" on board the *Lord Lowther* which arrived in Madras in May, for which seven of the ship's officers received gaol sentences. One would like to know much more of this "mutiny", for in 1810 there had been an army officers' mutiny of their "allowances for camp equipage" (a concession apparently never granted to subalterns), had seized Seringapatam and defied the Government of Madras.

One other detail of Wyndham Baker that these letters disclose, is his brief engagement to be married. Women in India rarely lacked suitors and, as the records show, remarried very speedily if their husbands died. In a letter dated 24th December 1838 he says: "I am engaged to spend tomorrow Christmas Day with some friends of mine who are but lately married, and only fancy the lady this day year I thought I was engaged to, but luckily for me it has turned out otherwise."

In a previous letter to his sister dated 25th September he had written "My Mother tells me not to joke about matrimony: tell her she can rest quite contented; only fancy, the young lady I proposed to is to be married on Monday and I am invited to the wedding, is not this coolness exemplified?"

His chances of active service were still remote. In a letter to his father dated 9th April 1839, he says, "We are going on very quietly as regards the War but are still anticipating war with Burmah which will commence about the end of the monsoon, and are gradually pouring troops into the country so that, when the business does commence, I suppose we shall have a right good conquest."

Action at Kurnoul

It was shortly after this in 1839 that Baker got his first chance of active service. In a letter to his sister (dated 27th August, sent by the overland mail by way of Suez and, for those days miraculously, received on 31st October), he writes that he is taking "a company of Artillery marching with the Infantry Regiments, to a place called Adony, about 150 miles from Secunderabad". At Adony they were to meet a force of "two squadrons of Dragoons, a regiment of Cavalry, two troops and companies of Artillery and six more infantry regiments moving "to the attack of the native fort of Kurnoul. They say the Rajahh is a very rich man who I do not despair of getting an allowance of Prize Money." He adds that his detachment needed "2,000 bullocks... in carrying the shot and shells besides no end in draft and numerous elephants and camels," so his train was long and unwieldy.

Actually Baker's hopes of fighting and prize money nearly foundered within the next three weeks. The monsoon was exceptional and the roads almost non-existent. "We frequently started at 4 a.m. and did not arrive at the encamping ground till noon," he writes to his mother from Kurnoul on 15th October, "added to this we had two rivers to cross... both much swollen by the late rains and about as broad as the Thames at London Bridge. The only boats available for crossing these large rivers were some basket ones, from 8 to 10 feet in diameter covered with leather; in these rickety things we were obliged to embark all our Park, Ordnance Stores, etc. Every wheeled carriage, gun, etc. had to be taken to pieces and carried to the boats and put together on the other side; at the first river after using our utmost endeavours we with difficulty got everything across in 10 days" and 20 lives were lost when one boat capsized against a rock.

"I began to feel the effects of such constant exposure and applied for medical advice. The Doctor pronounced me to be suffering from dysentery and said it must have been on me for some time... I was compelled to take to my bed and not allowed to stir except to be carried to my Dooly, which is an inferior kind of Palanquin used for the sick on a march."

One of the officers who attended him developed cholera which broke out "to an alarming extent just at the same time, of which numbers died daily. It did not contribute to raise my spirits, and from not taking anything but tea and toast and water, I was, before I had been taken ill a week, reduced to a mere skeleton."

It was 3rd October before the Secunderabad detachment joined up with the rest of the force "and really it was most magnificent the first view we had of the camp, it had the appearance of a large canvas lake," on the edge of the Rajah's territory, and 23 miles from Kurnoul. The reason for this imposing concentration of troops was a Wahabi called Ghulam Rasul Khan, "a man of weak mind, infatuated folly and extravagance, the result of his excessive sensualities", in Chitty's words. He bled his subjects almost white with taxation and according to the same writer once added 5,000 rupees to the revenue demand of a single village simply because one of his horses happened to die there! He maintained an immense harem, spent large sums on personal belongings and had been accumulating military stores and cannon in great quantities. Fearing a Wahabi conspiracy against the Government, a Commission was sent there with a large number of troops under Colonel Dyce "to overcome the Nabob".

The commission had reached Kurnoul on 12th September while Baker's detachment was still struggling along the road from Secunderabad. Weeks of parleying followed and finally the Commission gave Ghulam Rasul Khan till 5th October to hand over the fort of Kurnoul with all its military stores.

"On the morning of the 5th," Baker goes on, "he marched out of his fort and gave it up to us without a shot being fired. The Commissioner's escort quietly marched in and took possession and our Brigade marched on here from the other camp on the 10th and arrived in sight of Kurnoul on the 11th. We were heartily glad to receive the order to march on here as the cholera had again broken out in the old camp and six officers had died within a week – most of them after a few hours illness. It was perfectly heart-rending to see men dying in all directions. When the disease first broke out, there was not one case in 10 that did not prove fatal; since that many have escaped."

After further gossip about moves, Baker goes on rather inconsequently: "If you feel inclined to send me out anything by Place" (a brother officer apparently under orders for the East) "the following articles will prove most useful, one dozen of fine full-fronted shirts, half a dozen flannel waistcoats, three or four black silk neckerchiefs, and one dozen false collars, besides numerous little presents from the young ladies in the way of drawings etc." The young gunner was presumably looking forward to resuming his busy social life at Secunderabad. A letter written the next day (16th October) makes clear that "the business was nearly over", and the troops expected to be ordered back shortly to their cantonments.

This letter has much to say of the Nawab. "He positively declared his innocence and swore that he was most amicably inclined towards the Company" and even let two officers search the Fort. "They came back fully persuaded that the Nabob's story was true, but the business did not end there for two of the villain's own creatures came forward and turned evidence against their master. The agents went to the Nabob a second time and requested him to give up his fort for examination and the cunning rascal said he would go out the next day and let them search wherever they liked, never dreaming that his own people were evidence against him. The moment the agents had the Fort to themselves, the guides said 'Now we will show you everything', and the first place they went to was the Nabob's own Palace where they began digging and in the course of the day discovered 500 guns, powder, shot, shell, muskets and ammunition of every description, sufficient to equip 100,000 men. They must have been collecting for years. Unfortunately the Rajah was permitted to leave the Fort with all his private property so that is all lost to Government but of course they will keep his country, valued at 15 lakhs a year or about £150,000, his head will also be forfeited. He is now staying at his ancestor's tomb surrounded by all his troops who are clamorous for arrears of pay."

A letter among these papers, (dated 21st October 1839 and apparently written by an officer of the 13th Dragoons), adds more details about the hidden stores discovered in the Fort. Besides the "500 cannon" there were "50 field-pieces, all ready in every respect for field service: and elephant and camel batteries... Many of the guns are of brass made in the fort and never fired from and are very perfect and beautiful guns but some of a size perfectly absurd; among these is a new mortar made in the fort, 27½ inches inside the muzzle and the metal nine inches thick. The mortar in rear of the Horse Guards is a mere pocket pistol to it; so large indeed that ... had they attempted to fire it, it would have done more harm to friends than foes... Among the small-arms were 70 double-barrelled guns by Manton and other first-rate makers, all kept in most perfect order, and they were of different calibre, each had a bag containing 50 balls attached to the trigger guard."

The Nawab had meantime retired a mile from Kurnoul to a place called Jólapur (or Ghoranpur) where his troops guarded him in a walled enclosure which was his father's tomb. These troops were described by Chitty as "Rohillas and Arabs" but a letter from Baker says that they included Pathans, Baluchis and Afghans, all from the Northern Frontier of India and "considered the most faithful brave and best-equipped band of mercenaries to be met with in India."

They were however discontented, being owed considerable arrears of pay and they clamoured for it from the Nawab. However it is clear from Baker's letter (written to his sister Julia on his return to Secunderabad) on 18th November, that in the action on 18th October they fought well, "all the Rohilla chiefs being killed." Baker's account of his first action may speak for itself.

"We had a force of 800 fighting men, Foot and Horse Artillery, European and Native Cavalry, a few European Infantry, and a Regiment of native Sepoys, and were ordered to take the Nabob dead or alive. He, meanwhile had taken up his position in a tomb or Mosque completely surrounded by high walls, situated in a village about two miles from our camp."

"The whole ground had been reconnoitred by Colonel Dyce and his staff the evening before, a spot had been chosen for our guns and the whole plan of attack arranged without exciting the least suspicion amongst the Nabob's followers. At 4 a.m. of the 18th we had all fallen in, and until the order was given to load I do not think one 50th part of the men knew what was going to take place as our plans had been carried out with such secrecy. At sunrise the Commanding Officer rode forward to hold a conference with the Nabob; we had

drawn up to within half a gunshot range of them without their
knowledge, and Colonel Dyce found them unprepared for such a visit
as ours. He proceeded to inform the Nabob that he had come to take
him prisoner and that if his followers would give him up quietly we
would ensure their safety and give them their pay, if not after an
hour's time our guns would open fire on them. However they would
not listen to our terms and Colonel Dyce ordered us to move to
another position about 150 yards from the place occupied by the
Nabob; we were supported on either side by small portions of cavalry
and infantry and managed the move without opposition, but it was
rather an anxious hour. They numbered full three to two of us and
were known to be exceedingly brave fellows. As there was no chance
of averting bloodshed Colonel Dyce ordered us to open fire so we
kept up a regular shower of grape which at that short distance made
awful havoc, meanwhile some of them made a desperate charge on
the Infantry but were driven back to the Nabob's stronghold. We then
commenced shelling the tomb and after a few rounds had been fired
the building came knocking about their ears, then the Europeans and
native Infantry advanced to the charge and they were driven back at
the point of the bayonet. There was now a great struggle at the tomb
but British valour could not be withstood and the enemy were obliged
to fly. They were pursued by the cavalry and infantry and the
slaughter must have been great as 180 bodies were picked up the
following day on the banks of the river. The Nabob was taken
prisoner and all his elephants, horses and treasure fell into our hands
so nothing could be more complete than this little victory, the loss on
our side was not very great, two officers being killed and two more
wounded and amongst the men it was very small, thank God. So
ended the Battle of Goranpoor and many old soldiers who were
engaged in the affair said it was one of the smartest things they had
witnessed while it lasted. It is a very strange feeling for a novice like
myself to be for the first time in an engagement with the whizzing of
balls over your head, but the excitement is so great at times that it
makes one forget the danger.

"I took possession of a dagger found on one of the prisoners and
shall send it to my Mother as an ornament for her cabinet. They all
carry a matchlock, a sword, a brace of pistols, a dagger and a shield;

with the two first they are exceedingly expert and may be considered the best disciplined Troops in this part of the world.

"We were obliged to keep a pretty sharp lookout that night. The European soldiers picked up a great many valuable things, there was one case of an Englishman finding a large bag of Rupees. As much as 20 Rupees (£2) were offered by Europeans that night for a glass of brandy – Charley proving the truth of the old adage: 'Light come, light go'.

"The munitions of war inside the Fort were immense. If you have ever seen the Cadiz mortar in the Park (which I believe is the largest piece of ordnance in England) or heard of the monster which was used at Antwerp by the French, you may form some idea of the size of some of the guns found in the fort, when I tell you they would be considered playthings alongside those lately discovered. The sanguine think there is a chance of the Government giving the Fort up to us for Prize Money. If so I calculate my share would be four or five hundred pounds and if they only give the elephants to those who were engaged on the 18th, my share would be about £70, at any rate enough to pay my expenses during the march from Secunderabad and back again. A great quantity of jewels and coins have been discovered in the Fort; I visited the place the other day where they are being kept and could easily have taken a small bag full."

Ghulam Rasul Khan, the Nawab of Kurnoul who had caused all this trouble, was according to Chitty[1] sent down to Trichinopoly where, somewhat surprisingly, he became a Christian. One day however, after attending the chapel, he was assassinated by his own servant whom he had accused of theft. His former domain was later made into a regular district of Madras Presidency.

It may be noted from this letter that Baker returned to Secunderabad in about 18 days, presumably after the monsoon had ceased, compared with the 45 days which he took to reach Kurnoul. "What with the monsoon and dysentery I was heartily tired of the whole business." On 21st January 1840 he wrote to his father that he was proceeding at once to Madras, but was uncertain whether he would be posted to Moulmein in Burma or to Penang. War with

1. *Manual of the Kurnoul Dt. of the Presidency of Madras by N.G. Chitty, 1886.*

China was already looming, and he had just heard of Queen Victoria's wedding.

"Your English papers contain but little to interest us Indians. The Queen's marriage rather surprised us; I am glad she is going to be married more for my own sake than her's, as the Army will get a Brevet[1] by it, and we the Artillery will get three new Lt. Colonels.

"The Chinese are still anxious to be shown how Englishmen fight and I dare say will have a pretty lesson taught them before long. They forced two of our men-of-war to fire into their flanks the other day and the first discharge sunk several of their great and awkward ships. If I go to Penang I shall see lots of them as they treat a great deal with the people in that Settlement, and I may perhaps get sent there with the Artillery. We have felt the effects of the trade being stopped with China by the rise in tea, ginger etc. The former I used to get of excellent quality for two shillings a pound, now I pay about seven, so you may be prepared for a much great rise in England. We, the English, have commenced cultivating the Tea Plant in Assam and in a few years I dare say be able to meet our own demands. The Tea grown there is pronounced to be of a very superior quality and as it would be a great source of Revenue for our honourable master the East India Company, we ought to wish for their success. The Company are immense losers by the sale of Opium being prohibited in China and require some good thing to make up for their losses.

A soldier's life on the whole is full of novelty. Now I have a long tiresome march to Madras by myself and shall be full a month on my journey."

---

1. *An official document conferring certain privileges.*

Plans for the Chinese Expedition

Letter copied by one of the family, original lost.

St. Thomas' Mount,
March 21st, 1840.

I told you in my last [letter] of having been appointed to join the Chinese Expedition, and on my arrival here on the 14th found all as I could have wished it. Transports are all in the Roads for us and we are to embark in another fortnight; we proceed first to Singapore in the Straits of Malacca which has been appointed the rendezvous for us all. We shall probably be a month on our voyage there and shall not go on to China until the Fleets from England and Australia join us. You can hardly fancy what a deal of benefit I have derived from a change of air, combined with the excitement of preparation for this undertaking, my waking and sleeping dreams are of *the Land of Green Tea*![1] We are envied to a degree by the Artillery and Sappers, being the only ones going from this Presidency, but I do not think any ultimate advantage can be gained. Foreign powers must and will interfere if we enforce the Blockade and we generally think the Americans (who have some Men-of-War stationed there), will be the first to show their teeth, but our Fleet will be amply sufficient to keep them in check until fresh ships come to our succour. How long we may be away is a matter of extreme doubt, something between one and three years perhaps, but if they form a Colony on the Island of Formosa some of us will be left to garrison it, and then it may be many years 'ere we return to the Continent of India. I for one shall try to return as I don't like what I have heard of the climate. Do not take it for granted that we shall take possession of the island even, as the big whigs have only disclosed some of their intentions and I have stated general rumours on the subject.

We have a nice ship to take us over and if we have likeable weather I dare say the whole affair will be agreeable enough, but I am a shocking bad sailor. As it is expected that we shall have some land service we are obliged

---

1. *Note on Teas kindly sent to me by Matheson & Co. Ltd., 3 Lombard Street, London, E.C.3. Black Tea. Any tea that has been thoroughly fermented before being fired. Green Tea. Tea leaves that have been sterilized either in live steam, hot air or hot pans (whereby fermentation is prevented), and then rolled and dried.*

to take servants and some equipage with us. I have two of the former and one small tent; only the staff are permitted to take horses with them so my faithful beasts will change masters.

(Post Paid to Bombay. Cost 2/8d.   *Per Overland Mail)*

Mrs F. Baker,
Wylye Rectory,
Wiltshire,
United Kingdom.   St. Thomas' Mount,
April 12th, 1840. 10 p.m.

My dear Mother,

We go on board ship tomorrow and shall sail the following morning at latest.

To give you an idea of the hurry, bustle and confusion, I deem quite out of the question. We start from this in three hours and I have been working like a convict all day, getting the men and Troops ready for the voyage.

I have given one of the passengers, a particular friend of the name of Heriot, charge of two daggers which I took at Gooranpore, which I send you as curiosities.

The Transport we sail in is the *Rustomjee Cowasjee*,[1] 750 tons, with a Lascar crew of 90 men. Into this little vessel they are going to cram 12 officers, 230 European soldiers, and 240 Native Troops and followers, so we shall have a good deal to look to in getting through the Straits of Malacca which is very bad navigation in this season of the year. With a crowded ship

---

1. From *"The Dictionary of Indian Biography"*, we learn that Rustomji Cowasji was a merchant prince in his day, head of the firm of Rustomji Cowasji & Co. of Calcutta. His son Rustomji Manackji joined the firm in Calcutta in 1837 which built the 'opium clippers' to China.
From Basil Lubbock's *"The Opium Clippers"*, we hear that the Rustomjee Cowasjee was launched from the Kidderpore Dock on July 12, 1839, "one of the finest craft ever built, 764 tons, and like the Sylph and Cowasjee Family had been specially designed for her owner Sir Robert Seppings."
The Rustomjee Cowasjee acted as a hired transport in the Opium War, though she occasionally carried opium.
So far I have not been able to find a picture of her and perhaps it is because her life was short. There is a small, sad entry saying that she left Calcutta on June 23rd, 1850, with a cargo worth 800,000 dollars, then she passed Singapore on July 26 and went missing.

we have many worries to solve, things to dread, but I say to myself: 'Fear not but trust in Providence, wherever thou may'st be.' Do you remember the Pilot's Song, of which the above is the chorus?

THE PILOT

Oh, Pilot, 'tis a fearful night!
There's danger on the Deep;
I'll come and pace the deck with thee
I do not care to sleep.
'Go down! go down!' the Pilot cried,
'This is no place for thee,
Fear not but trust in Providence
Wherever thou may'st be.'

Ah Pilot! Dangers often met
We all are apt to slight,
And thou has known these raging waves,
But to subdue their might;
'It is not apathy,' he cried,
'That gives this strength to me
Fear not but trust in Providence
Wherever thou mayst be.'

'In such a storm the sea engulfed
My Father's lifeless form;
My only brother's boat when down
In such a cruel storm;
And such perhaps may be my lot!
Yet still I say to thee,
Fear not but trust in Providence
Wherever thou mayst be.'

Kindly sent in answer to my letter in the *Observer*, by Mr J. Shearman, 6a St. John's Road, Isleworth, Middlesex, who remembered the Pilot's Song by heart; this was some time between 1936 and 1939.

N.B. I am told the Pilot's Toast is: 'Deep draft ships and plenty of water under them!'

Letter from Wyndham written to:-

Miss H.A. Baker,
Wylye Rectory,
Wiltshire.
Post Paid to Bombay   Per Overland Mail via Falmouth.

Ship Postage 0. 2. 0.
Inland Postage 0.14.0.

(There is a note on the envelope saying: "October 6th received" – in which case this letter took nearly five months!)

At Sea.Straits of Malacca.

Lat. 1" 53 N. Long. 102" 7 E.

May 14th, 1840.

My dear Harriett,

I am now within a few days sail of our destination, the Island of Singapore. I shall commence a letter to you, fill it by degrees, and despatch it by the first opportunity that offers.

Our ship, the *Rustomjee Cowasjee*, is the property of a very rich Parsee Merchant in Calcutta, of the same name as the ship, which will account to you for its being so uncommon, she is quite new and considered a fine strong built ship. Besides the Captain we have two European officers and a crew of 85 Bengal Lascars, who are tolerable industrious seamen in fine weather, but they have neither the moral or physical strength of our own Jack Tars to stand much boisterous weather.

I told you we should be much crowded, but I never had so much as a thought that we should be crowded to the extent we really are. We muster 216 Europeans, 250 natives and upwards, and including every person on board the party amounts to 550 souls. The consequence is that we look more like a slaver than a Transport, and in bad weather the decks are so blocked up that it is dangerous to work the ship. Our party at the Cuddy Table[1] consists of 14, and of course we are tolerably off, but still our state admits of improvement, and we hope to get another ship at Singapore to

---

1. *A* Cuddy *was a small cabin or cook-room, generally in the fore part of a boat or lighter. In large vessels the name* Cuddy *referred to the Captain's cabin under the poopdeck. In this case the Cuddy was probably the Captain's Table. (Taken from an old dictionary in Trinity House.)*

take one half of our troops on board. The Europeans, poor fellows! are very ill-used – imagine 6 ft by 1 ft 2 ins for an ablebodied man to sleep in. The Government were not aware of our state or we should have been detained in Madras.

Now for the voyage up to this date. We have been most unfortunate in wind and weather; for six consecutive days we hardly had anything but strong bad weather and were knocking about in the Bay of Bengal in a most horrible way with a very heavy disagreeable sea. We sighted land for the first time on the 28th when we came bang on the Island of Cunicabar without knowing the least where we were. The fact is that the weather had been bad for so long that we had no opportunity of making any observations, and our reckoning was considerably out of calculation. The rain only held up for a few minutes when land was discovered, this was at noon, had it been 12 hours later none of us would have been alive to tell the tale.

May 12th, 1840.

We have several ships in sight today, and one is reported to be a packet to Calcutta, so I hurry this letter in case we should fall in with her.

We went into Malacca on the 9th to get refreshments. It was formerly a Portuguese Settlement and became the property of the Dutch, who afterwards exchanged it with us for the Island of Java. Even in England I never saw a place look so deliciously verdant and refreshing as this; all places after a long voyage look nice but this took my fancy amazingly. The pines[1] were most beautiful here and I thought I should never be able to leave off eating them, they were selling at less than a halfpenny a piece, ones that would fetch at least £1 in Covent Garden Market. We also found some very nice preserves here, and some which I am sure you would relish exceedingly, but it is no use making your mouth water for things which it is totally out of my power to send you. I only purchased a few sticks of a kind that can only be got here, called the Malacca Cane, and shall get them handsomely mounted in China, and one of these days hope they will be the property of some of my friends at home.

The population of Malacca is principally Chinese, the natives of the place are Malays, so it was in every way quite new to me. The Chinese are very funny fellows and I was glad to have an opportunity of seeing them, you can rarely judge of them from the accounts you read. They are much more

1. *He means pineapples*

intelligent and better looking than I supposed. I had a long conversation with a very clever and superior Chinaman, who had been for many years resident at Malacca and spoke English very tolerably. He said he had read a good deal about us and knew our power, but resented the idea of our attempting anything against his country. I told him we should be better judges in a few more months. He thought we must be fools for rushing headlong to destruction and that our days were numbered.

We have a few Companies of Infantry, and a detachment of Artillery at Malacca. Some of the officers I had met before and they were most hospitable – quite the Indian style of things. Four of the principal residents had dinners laid for a dozen, and we might all have been feasted for a month had we been able to remain here, but that could not possibly be managed, and we sailed accordingly yesterday morning.

We have been cramming on every stitch of canvas to catch up the Packet but it's no use, so I shall take my time and finish this letter at my ease.

We have fallen in with several of the Bengal Transports with the Queen's 26th[1] and 29th[2] on board, the rest we shall find at Singapore when we arrive. We shall all disembark at Singapore and wait for the English Fleet, and possibly proceed towards Canton about the beginning of next month; of this I shall be able to speak with more certainty when we get there.

Whilst we remain on board our expenses are comparatively nothing, as we have everything provided for the sum of two Rupees a day. The Government, with their usual liberality, make up the difference to the Captain of the vessel and pay him six Rupees a day for each of us, so there's no excuse for our not being well looked after; 16/-s. a day per officer is a very handsome allowance.

When we get on shore our expenses increase enormously, but I hope our Chinese Prize Money will cover everything and leave something in hand. I left only two boxes behind at Madras so that my stock (both alive and dead) is much reduced by this trip.

I see you say in your last communication that Place is thinking of venturing to India about the end of April. If he has any taste he will endeavour to get some young lady to accompany him out here, as there is a much better chance for him at home than out here, where *nice young ladies* are exceedingly few and far between, and England is the only place after all to select a companion for life.

If you want a good book on China to read, get Downing's 'Stranger in

1. *The Cameronians.*
2. *The Worcestershires.*

China', you will find it one of the best yet written on the subject, and will give you a good insight into Chinese affairs and prepare you for some of the wondrous tales I shall be sending you one of these days.

Singapore Roads,
May 15th, 1840.

These Roads present the most animated sight I ever witnessed, Men-of-War, Steamers, Transports, Chinese Junks, and numerous native craft crowded together, and if it were not for the two last I might easily fancy myself at Portsmouth or Plymouth.

I thought it possible that we might have remained here some three weeks or a month, but the Admiral[1] declares we must be ready for the sea by the 20th, so we have only a few days to get things in order. However, I do not think it possible that we can start so soon as many of the Bengal Troops are still waiting and the ships from England are not forthcoming, so I trust we shall have to wait for them as I have many things to get which I had overlooked before leaving Madras. I have fallen in with many old friends here who are all bothering me to come on shore, but we are obliged to remain on board by turns to keep our men in order or there would be a pretty business in no time. However, I got on shore last evening for a few hours and was much amused with the different style of things to what I have been used to. The Wellesley's Band was playing on the Esplanade and all the society of the place turned out to witness the fun. Although this is purely an English Settlement there are numerous Dutch and Portuguese families, and the English are, of course, the leaders of the fashion amongst the better class of society, but people of every nation in Europe wear pretty much their own national dresses and certainly the collection is most entertaining.

Ladies go about in their carriages without either caps or bonnets, and some with merely a long veil hanging down gracefully over their shoulders, but of these things I will tell you more fully in my next.

We do not even know who is to command the Expedition, but expect to hear something by every ship that arrives. Sir Gordon Bremer is now the

---

1. *Rear-Admiral Sir Gordon Bremer.*

Senior Naval Officer, but they say Admiral Elliot[1] (from New South Wales) is coming round to supersede him immediately. This is therefore the cause of our being in such haste to get away before he arrives. I am still pretty certain that we shall be away from Madras a couple of years at least, for if it once comes to fighting no one can tell where it will end, and no one who knows anything of the subject doubts for a moment that the Chinese will refuse to accept our terms, as everyone knows what an obstinate race of beings we have to deal with.

On Board the *Rustomjee Cowasjee*,
Lat: 22, Long: 113.
Sunday, June 21st, 1840.

To his sister Louisa,

We are at this moment within 45 miles of the Portuguese Settlement of Macao and have lots of little islands on all sides in sight, but the plans of the Commodore have not yet transpired, and we are now lying-to while he has gone on in a War Steamer to reconnoitre. We shall therefore not anchor till tomorrow evening and the following day I think the Artillery will commence their part in the morning's play, so we are all impatience as you may suppose.

The following seems to be the general opinion and I dare say not far from the correct one:- viz. that our terms will be rejected with contempt, that the Men-of-War will then batter away at the Forts on the Canton River, and when they are breached, the Military will land to take possession. These fools will then be garrisoned by us to co-operate with the Navy in enforcing the strictest Blockade. If this does not bring them to reason we shall then go direct against Canton, which is not above 20 miles above the Forts alluded to – and now you know as much about it is we do ourselves.

We have been fully occupied this last week in getting all things in immediate readiness for landing, and when once we have our guns on terra

---

1. *Rear-Admiral Sir Gordon Bremer acted as Naval C.-in-C. until the arrival of Rear-Admiral George Elliot, who took over again in November 1840, when George Elliot was invalided. Bremer was eventually relieved in August 1841, by Admiral Sir William Parker.*

firma, the worst part of the bargain is over, as it takes some considerable time and labour to get them out of the boats, and put them together for Service.

We are opposed to 20 times our Force as far as numbers go, but they are infinitely inferior to us in every other way. However I hope before I finish this to be able to say that the British Standard floats on the walls of the 'Boca Tigris',[1] and that our loss has been very inconsiderable.

Our voyage from Singapore has been better than that from Madras; the weather delightful with nice smooth water the whole way and I shall really be quite sorry when it ends. The number of ships in company with us adds considerably to our amusement as we are continually signalling and in calm weather paying each other visits.

We left some Men-of-War and a steamer at Singapore to bring up the remainder of the transports. I expect your letters will be forwarded by this opportunity, so I am anxiously hoping for their arrival.

The island of Singapore is small but exceedingly pretty and like all the other islands in the Straits of Malacca, covered with pine trees down to the water's edge. As far as freshness and verdure goes, Malacca, in my opinion, has the advantage; but as the former is very thriving, and the other the contrary, they will not bear comparison, except in beauty. The population is mostly Chinese with a sprinkling of Madras people and some native Malays; the first being by far the most industrious, have nearly the whole employment of the island, while the remainder seem to live by fishing. The society of the place is but very limited and is mostly composed of American, Dutch, French, Portuguese and a second-class type of English merchant – of the latter I can only speak, not having met any of the others save the American Consul who gave us a Ball. These generally live in a very handsome style with capital houses and all the in-door comforts to correspond, but their horses and equipage are the most paltry you ever beheld, as they cannot contrive by any means to get horses to live on the island and are therefore obliged to substitue handy little Java ponies. Spices of all sorts, and the nutmeg in particular, grow to perfection, while the beautiful shrubs contribute greatly to the beauty of the place.

The finest turtles and fish of all sorts are caught in abundance and the island produces the choicest fruits; still, with all these good things John Bull cannot help grumbling at the scarcity of beef and mutton (just like the majority of Britishers who will stick to the same old things they have been

1.   *The 'Boca Tigris' was the Chinese Fort at the entrance of the Canton River.*

brought up on, and eaten for years, rather than be adventurous and try the specialities of a new land), which at times cannot be procured for love or money! They have tried every method to rear these animals also on the island, but directly the wet weather commences they die off to a certainty, but this very season is considered most healthy. When we were there the Commissariat had purchased cattle from all parts, at an enormous price for the use of this Expedition, and when we left they were dying off 20 or 30 a day, and I am sure one out of 40 will be turned to account in making salt junk for our Troops!

As Singapore is the Madras Botany Bay, nearly all the public roads and buildings have been constructed by the convicts, at little or no expense to the Government. The shopkeepers are a very extraordinary independent set of people and consider they are doing you a favour in selling you any of their articles, altho' they make no hesitation in charging you a dollar where half would be ample, and if you don't look out will shake you by the hand the next time you meet. They all make a complete harvest out of us and I dare say will be glad enough to see us again when we return.

At Singapore I lived with a fellow-passenger and friend of mine called Baldwin who is a barrister, and comfortably settled. He did all he could to amuse me when duty permitted me to be away from my ship. I met at his house a Bengal Merchant who married a Miss Brice, and had been most fortunate lately in an African speculation, having made £60,000 clear in five months, and also by the sale of that drug[1] in China. He told me he expected his firm would give him £20,000 more to retire and then he intended going home for good. He is little more than 30 and has been a very short time in the country. I mention this as a case of extraordinary luck; although immense fortunes are accumulated by the great merchants, the Military men never have the same chance, as by the regulations of the Service we are prohibited from trading in any way.

We generally pass away the long evenings with a rubber of whist and it often reminds me of our little parties at home, as we only play for amusement and everyone tries to make himself as amusing as he can, so we have a continual round of passes and are all as merry as possible. One old Colonel who is a nice old soldier, enjoys it as much as the youngest, that's myself, so we have a very agreeable party.

I met at Singapore a Captain Brooke[2], formerly of our Service, but having

1. *Opium*
2. *Captain Sir James Brooke (1803–68) the famous traveller, also became Rajah of Sarawak, and was helped by a kindred spirit – Sir Henry Keppel – in his efforts to put down the numerous pirates who infested the seas near Borneo.*

a large fortune left him, retired; and is now moving about in this part of the world in his yacht, exploring islands along the coast of Java, which have never before been visited by Europeans. He always has a Doctor, an astronomer, and a few other scientific men accompanying him, and in this manner spends his whole income of course – £5,000 or £6,000 a year. He intends publishing his disclosures and they will be invaluable to all navigators in these Seas.

NOTE ON OPIUM.

Mr Hsin-pao Chang in his book "Commissioner Lin and the Opium War", says on Page 49:

"Had it not been for the opium, bullion would have seeped out of Britain in exchange for tea, which in the 1830s furnished the Exchequer with three and a half million pounds sterling." The significance of opium may be further illustrated by a dispatch from Captain Elliot to Lord Palmerston, from Macao on February 2, 1837, which states that the value of British imports of opium into China in the proceeding year amounted to nearly 18 million dollars, about 1 million dollars in excess of the value of tea and silk exported during the same period on all British accounts. A keen and careful observer, Elliot was reluctant to see British commerce and capital become so heavily dependent upon 'the steady continuance of a vast prohibited traffic in an article of vicious luxury, high in price, and liable to frequent and prodigious fluctuation'."

But the stakes were too high for the British to abandon the trade. The Duke of Wellington declared in May 1838 that, far from looking gloomily upon this opium trade, Parliament had cherished it, suggested its extension, and had deliberately looked for means of promoting it. It is therefore not without justification that Jardine, the leading opium merchant, shortly before his departure from Canton on January 26, 1839, defended himself and his fellow traders:

"I hold, gentlemen, the society of Canton high: it holds a high place in my opinion, even among the merchants of the East; yet I also know that this community has often heretofore and lately been accused of being a set of smugglers. This I distinctly deny; we are not smugglers, gentlemen! It is the Chinese Government, it is the Chinese officers who smuggle, and who connive at and encourage smuggling; not we:

and then look at the East India Company – why, the father of all smuggling and smugglers is the East India Company."

Similarly, Blackwood's Magazine concluded: "The sin of the opium trade, if sin there be, rests not with British merchants, but is divisible, in about equal proportions betwixt the Chinese and British Governments and the East India Company."

On Page 104 of his book Mr Chang says: "In the latter part of 1837, the vigorous measures of the provincial authorities effectively crushed the native smuggling networks at the outside anchorages of Canton and its immediate neighbourhood, but there was the side effect of a phenomenal increase in the traffic on the east coast of Kwangtung and the coast of Fukien."

Elliot reported on November 19: "Till within the last few months, that branch of the trade on the coast of eastern Kwangtung and Fukien never afforded employment to more than two or three small vessels; but, at the date of this despatch, and for some months past, there have not been less than 20 sail of vessels on the east coasts; and I am sorry to add, that there is every reason to believe blood has been spilt in the interchange of shot which has ever and anon taken place between them and the Mandarin boats."

The price of opium drastically declined: Patna was about 620 dollars per chest, Benares 560 dollars, and Malwa 445 dollars at the end of the year. In January, Patna and Benares suffered a further decline of a hundred dollars. In February, Malwa and Benares could be purchased at 400 dollars or lower and new Patna at 450 dollars. Jardine, whose firm held the greater part of Malwa in China, remarked, perhaps with a sigh: "Canton never was in so dull and distressed a state since I have know it. Not a ship loading for England, not a pound of Tea purchased for the Europe, or English markets; and very little for America.

At Sea off Buffalo Island
(Ning-po).
July 2nd, 1840.

When I commenced this letter we were lying off Macao and in immediate expectation of being ordered up to the Canton River to storm and take the Chinese Forts on its banks. Well, after tacking about in the same part for three days and upwards, a Man-of-War came out to tell us to betake ourselves to this island and to remain here till further instructions from the Commodore.[1] The distance is about 1,000 miles, this we accomplished in seven days, and after a very favourable voyage anchored here on the last day of June. This part of the China Seas is seldom visited by our countrymen, and therefore we were obliged to be very particular in navigating through these narrow and intricate passages. Numbers of Chinese came out in thin boats and looked at us and I dare say they never beheld such a sight in their lives before. They were evidently suspicious of us and would not be prevailed upon to fetch us provisions or hold any communication with us. The country looks exceedingly barren, although the poor inhabitants seem to cultivate every spot which is likely to yield a return; not a tree is visible in any direction and the only thing which appears to thrive is the sweet potato, with which you in England are unacquainted. The climate is very different from that of India and the thermometer does not vary very much above 80° at any time. The nights are quite cool and delightful. We are now in the same latitude as the Canary Islands, but much colder in the winter, as during the N.E. wind the ice comes down from Kamsihasha and is very abundant at this season.

Much to our surprise the Commodore joined us yesterday with two War steamers and a few of the slow-sailing transports, which had dropped astern of us in the voyage from Singapore; with them came the following intelligence: The Commodore after holding several conferences with the Chinese authorities, found that his offers were treated with contempt, and that it was quite unavailing to attempt coming to terms. He therefore proclaimed a Blockade with China and left several Men-of-War to carry his orders into effect, every vessel belonging to the Chinese will therefore be captured, as trading boats alone are to pass unmolested. The moment this order was made known Lin[2] put 10,000 Dollars on Captain Elliot's head.

---

1. *Rear-Admiral George Elliot.*
2. *Lin Tse-hsu was Chinese Imperial Commissioner at Canton.*

The Blockade if strictly enforced will be felt most severely by the Chinese, and the Americans are not likely to be over well pleased about it, however it was the only resource he could adopt and the sooner they are made to feel their inability to cope with us, the sooner they will be inclined to come to terms.

The English Fleet must be very near Macao by now so they will have complete command of the sea.

To return to our own movements, we – I mean the Land Force – with six Men-of-War and two steamers, are making the best of our way to the large Island of Chusan, which we can hardly reach until tomorrow morning as it is about 30 miles to our northward. The Island we seize at once as it is in a most capital position for annoying the Chinese, we shall probably keep possession of it until the affair is at an end. We expect some opposition on the part of the inhabitants and when we are well settled there, shall be frequently visited by the Chinese soldiers who will use every endeavour to retake the Island. It is about 30 miles long by 15 broad, with a very large population and extensive trade with Nanking and Ningpo. Our taking possession of this place is a most politic move as it divides their attention between Canton and Nanking. The latter place we can easily make an attack on if we feel inclined, as the River Yangtse-Kiang is one of the largest in China and nearly navigable as far as Nanking; so they are now in rather a disagreeable predicament and if wise will accept our offers before things become more disastrous.

Admiral Elliot, Captain Elliot, and Sir G. Bremer, have been appointed Plenipotentiaries, and Lord Jocelyn Secretary for the settlement of these affairs in China. The first is the *Melville*, which is expected immediately. I fear none of the three are eminent men, and with the exception of the second are quite unacquainted with Chinese affairs. Brigadier Bartley of the 18th Royal Irish commands the Land Force and is much on a par with the others, only rather more of an old woman if anything. Lord J. Churchill, Commander of the *Druid*, and Major-General Oglander have died lately, both gallant fellows, and better gifted for the command of this Expedition than the others.

We are fairly booked for two or three months here as until the N.E. Monsoon sets in, it will be impossible for a sailing vessel to get to the southward. This will not be before September and after that none can work here; so we are cut off from all communication with our friends at Macao and Singapore, except by steam. My letters will therefore become scarcer which is one of the few disagreeable attending this business.

The Land of Green Tea

Note on green tea by courtesy of Stephen Kist of Christie's:

"Green tea is a Far Eastern tea. Instead of roasting the tea leaves, as is usual in Europe, green tea consists of steamed tea leaves, which allows them to stay of a strong green colour.

In Continuation, Saturday, July 11th, 1840.
Island of Chusan.

In consequence of entrance into this harbour being exceedingly intricate, the Commodore judged it expedient to dispatch a steamer to take a survey of it, before the remainder of the Fleet; while therefore this was being carried forward we were lying at anchor some leagues off, and we may consider it exceedingly fortunate that the passage was not attempted at first, as if it had been no doubt many of the vessels would have been lost.

On the morning of the 3rd the steamer *Atlanta* was sent to execute the above survey; on her return we learned that she had been once on shore and had also struck on a rock on her way thither. This was a bad beginning but it was for our benefit, as her damages were but slight, compared to what ours might have been had we gone straight at it at once. The *Wellesley*[1] 74 with some other Men-of-War got in that evening, but the whole of the Transports remained outside and we were not all at anchor in the Harbour of China till 2 a.m. on Sunday, July 5th.

At this time we were about three quarters of a mile from the Shore Batteries and in rear of the Men-of-War, who were in a line between us and the shore. The day before, when the *Wellesley* was first in the harbour, she had immediately been visited by the Mandarins and chief authorities of the Island, who were informed by the Interpreter of our proposals and the absolute necessity for the place being given up to us. The Mandarins stated

1. In June *1840, the Royal Naval Squadron, including the* Wellesley, *had halted off the Great Zadrones to communicate with Macao, before proceeding north to Chusan. –From the "Royal Naval History of the War."*

Map of the Canton River.
Published by courtesy of Messrs. Brown Son & Ferguson Ltd, Glasgow, S.I.

that if we dared to offer any opposition the Emperor, their Master, would not hesitate to take off our heads; but when they were acquainted of our determination to take possession of the place and of our ability to help ourselves, they appeared tacitly to consent. However, we told them that we should land at a certain hour on the following day whatever happened. The Conference was thus concluded.

The moment we were all collected at anchor, the signal was hoisted for the Troops to embark in the boats in the order previously agreed upon. At this time there was a considerable number of persons assembled on a hill overlooking the harbour and apparently making preparations for opposing us. The whole of the boats belonging to the Transports as well as the Men-of-War were put in requisition to land the men; and when they were loaded with as many men as they could carry they moved off some buoys where it was arranged they should collect, till the whole of the Troops were in readiness to start for the shore.

The leading boats were appropriated to the 18th Royal Irish and the Marines who were directed to cover our landing. A shot from the *Wellesley* announced to the Chinese the expiration of their time for deliberation. An anxious moment followed, and to the astonishment of those who knew that the Mandarins were already acquainted with the fearful odds against them, the Batteries on shore and the War Junks discharged their insignificant broadsides.

The Bay, which was full of boats hastening on shore with the Troops, now rang with a deafening shout, which was instantly drowned in the roar of the Artillery from the *Wellesley, Conway, Allington, Algerine, Atlanta* and *Battlesnake*, and all was smoke and noise for a quarter of an hour. The fire from the enemy was nearly harmless, indeed their knowledge of Artillery was so inferior and their ordnance of such rude description that we had nothing to fear from them; but the heavy fire from the Men-of-War told fearfully on the inoffensive inhabitants and destroyed their Junks,[1] Guns and Batteries. A few minutes after the firing from the shipping had ceased, the boats with the advance Troops landed unopposed, and the place where the Chinese had assembled before the action was now deserted. A Jack Tar mounted to the top of their flag-staff, hauled down the Imperial Flag of the celestial Empire, and the Union Jack of England was quickly flying in its stead. Two of our guns now landed, followed by the Bengal Regiment of Volunteers, the 4th Queen's and the reserve of Artillery. I was attached to

---

1. *"Junk" from junco which has a Javanese origin.*

the latter, but of course had many a senior to claim the Post of Honour in the advance and, nolens volens, was obliged to submit.

The town was quickly deserted but we soon found they had made their escape to a large city about a mile from the beach which is wholly unseen from the Bay and we had therefore never heard of it before. This town was soon discovered to be well fortified and we hastened to a position 500 yards from their walls, from whence we kept up a slow fire of shrapnel and shell, to which they replied by a similar compliment.

By nine o'clock that night we had 12 guns and four mortars in Battery, which was no easy task I can assure you considering the shipping, unshipping, and the dragging of them over a mile of the worst and narrowest road. This was all done by our men and you can imagine how delighted we were to knock off for the night with the belief that our hard work would be turned to some account next morning. Of course it was an anxious night and we were all obliged to bivouac round a large fire, equipped for immediate service.

We had one or two alarms but none of any consequence. The town with the Batteries, between us and the shipping, caught fire during the night and was extinguished with the utmost difficulty.

The Engineers went forward, at early dawn, to reconnoitre the Fort and prepare for storming it; what was their surprise to find it had been evacuated during the night. The town was immediately taken possession of and strong guards placed over the public buildings to prevent its recapture.

I am sorry to say the following day the Troops were plundering in every direction and nothing could restrain them. The fact was, that the old town which had first been attacked – in fact all the towns – abounded in a spirit very common in China called Shumshoo. (It is extracted from rice and is a pernicious liquor!) This could not be kept out of the reach of the men and its effect on them was of the most dreadful nature and very different from that of the spirits we are used to in England. A man no sooner took a small quantity than he was bereft of his senses and men were lying about in all directions in a most dreadful state and committing the most horrible atrocities, which I am sorry to say are but too common in War. Since then we have been destroying every drop we can get hold of, and I think one day I must have destroyed some 20 hogshead of this pernicious liquor.

The Chinese, except as regards the use of Opium[1], are exceedingly

---

1. *The Dutch, who were masters of Formosa from 1624 to 1662, introduced opium to China; used with tobacco it was a natural resource against malaria. From Formosa the habit had spread through Amoy to the mainland.*

temperate in their habits and we cannot account for the intense distilleries which have been discovered here.

To-morrow we shall have been in quiet possession of the principal town on the Island for a week, without any attempt on the part of the Chinese to retake it. The inhabitants have been used most kindly by us and we use every endeavour to conciliate them; so I dare say in a few weeks they will have nearly all returned to their deserted homes. We have taken but little valuable Booty, indeed the destruction of the greater part of the town by fire, probably accounted for this.

The interior of the Island is more extensive than we originally thought, though much of it still remains unexplored. The country in our neighbourhood is most highly cultivated. Peaches, grapes, pears and plums and many more of your English fruits and vegetables grow here to perfection, and I dare say when the native Chinese people begin to understand our ways the Markets will be plentifully supplied.

Quadrupeds of all kinds are very scarce, a dozen ponies, as many bullocks and a few goats, are all we have yet seen, but poultry and fish abound. Rice, wheat and lots of other grains grow well, so we shall not starve with the occasional provision ship from India. Tea is very common in its dried state but I cannot say whether I have yet seen it growing in the fields.

The Fort is rather a strong one for these parts – only think we found an old English gun in one of the Batteries made by John Pearse in 1601 – how many tales it could tell of the Service that it has witnessed since then.

The *Melville* 74 with Admiral Elliot[1] and his relative Captain Elliot of Macao, came in a day or two after we took possession of the place. She had the misfortune to strike on the rock before alluded to at the entrance to the harbour, and I fear she will be unfit for any Service until she has been overhauled. The *Blonde* from England came in the day before yesterday, she touched on her way hither at Amoy. The interpreter landed to make them some offers about future trade. He was immediately fired on and the

---

1. *Admiral Sir George Elliot was Supreme Commander of the combined Forces, until he resigned owing to illness, which left his cousin Capt. Charles Elliot as sole Plenipotentiary.*
   The Admiral in his Memoirs speaks of what he calls "authorized smuggling"; how the Opium Ships sailed up rivers in broad daylight, and the Chinese paid the duty on the Opium under the noses of their own Forts. He had seen Dutch, American, Swedish and Danish Opium vessels besides our own, and if the trade with India was abolished Java alone could have supplied China with Opium. However, the trade was too lucrative to be abolished.

boat returned to the ship. Then she opened fire on the Fort and kept it up for two hours knocking the whole to pieces.

The accounts of the taking of this place and the Canton Blockade will most likely reach Peking about the same time, so the poor Emperor will be puzzled to know in which direction to turn his attention.

I have been into several public buildings in the Fort. The furniture is generally of the most elegant and comfortable description; and the dresses, which in their hurried state they left behind them, are most superb. Many of these have fallen into our hands and I have one at this moment in my possession, of a most costly description, embroidered all over very tastefully, which one day I hope to transfer to your collection.

It appears that the Emperor sets the fashion, through six months of the year he wears warm things and for the remainder, cool; of course varying in the texture according to their owners' wealth, some splendid silks and satin dresses lined with fur are amongst these wardrobes. Their Treasury must have been plundered 'ere we took possession as little or no silver is forthcoming.

We are now talking of taking Ningpo, a place of great importance on the mainland, not many leagues from this, and some Ships of War are now on a cruise up there to see if it is commendable for the large ships. Vague reports have reached us of a large army being collected there to oppose our invasion, which is quite likely, or it may be for an attempt to rescue their fair Island of Chusan.

I do not see a possibility of our being withdrawn, or of the business being settled for many months; indeed the authorities are at this moment consulting upon the expediency of building temporary Barracks for us here, against the cold season. This will be highly necessary in the event of our remaining here, as snow and ice in the winter are nearly as plentiful here as they are with you. The accounts you have heard and read of concerning the smallness of the ladies' feet in China are by no means exaggerated, as I have seen several so small that nothing would have persuaded me of it, had not mine eyes beheld them. It is more of a deformity than otherwise, as the part which actually belongs to the foot in its natural state, is punched up into the ankles and it gives them the most ugly appearance imaginable.

Chusan. July 19th, 1840.

Matters are nearly at a standstill here. The Admiral, they say, makes a move in a few days in the *Wellesley*, to the northward. As he takes nearly all the smaller vessels of War and steamers with him, we imagine that he thinks of running up the Peiho River as near Peking as he can go, but when he gets there nothing can be done without Troops, so we are in a state of the same uncertainty as ever.

The *Melville*'s services are at an end for the next six weeks while she is overhauled. It will not be unamusing perhaps to you, to have the names of the Naval Squadron at this station. Those marked with a cross are expected but have not yet arrived. *Wellesley* 74, *Blenheim* 74 (x), *Blonde* 46, *Druid* 46, *Pique* 36 (x), *Volage* 28, *Conway* 28, *Alligator* 28, *Andromache* 28 (x), *Nimrod* 20 (x), *Pearl* 20 (x), *Palades* 18, *Cruisee* 18, *Hyacinth* 18, *Algerine* 10.

I have as yet had little communication with the natives of this place; they certainly appear a strange people and widely different from the rest of the world. Their habits are exceedingly filthy and yet all their houses are comfortably furnished, and they certainly seem much better off than the poor in our country, and I should say they are far more addicted to vice than the most servile class of our countrymen. They are, it is said, accomplished in the arts of stealing, lying and deceit.

Perhaps for many months it will be our doom to remain here, indeed I half suspect that our Government will do all they can to retain possession of this Island for good, and only relinquish it as a last resort to pacify the Chinese. The honest Company (East India Company) whose servant I am, have nothing to do with the cost of the War, I am glad to say, the whole expense of it will be debited to the Queen. Her Troops will therefore garrison it and all will be allowed to return to India.

A steamer has arrived from Macao, she brought but little news. The Canton River is blockaded and our Men-of-War have taken a few Junks. If only we had struck sharp and heavy at all the places along the coast up here, but this time the Emperor himself would have been trembling in his shoes, and glad to come to whatever terms we proposed.

Portrait of Lin Tse-hsu.
by kind permission of the Berry-Hill Galleries, New York, U.S.A.

Post Paid to Bombay.   *Per Overland Mail via Suez.*

Postmark, Wylye, March 12th, 1841 – hence this letter took nearly seven months!

Chusan,
August 21st, 1840.

My dear Father,

Yesterday brought in the *Nimrod* with a large packet and I was most fortunate in receiving two letters from Wylye of the 2nd of April and May, their contents afforded me the greatest pleasure, your continued indisposition was the sole alloy but I am inclined to hope the summer has contributed much to your recovery.

This will be a long and expensive War you may depend on it. The Chinese have molested us very little since our occupation of the place. One well was found poisoned but luckily it was discovered before anyone partook of the water. A dog died in two minutes on drinking some of it, so we have since had sentries posted over the wells and it is not likely to occur again. High rewards have been offered by the Mandarins for European Heads,[1] but none of the rascals have yet attempted to possess themselves of that very valuable commodity. Lin, when he heard of the taking of this place, sent down 200 armed boats from Macao to capture the Men-of-War lying there, but after a little consideration they deemed it advisable to return without making the attempt.

Silver had been flowing out of China to pay for the opium or "foreign mud," as it was called, and this loss of specie had finally induced the Tao-Kuang Emperor, "the Son of Heaven", or more literally "Glorious Rectitude,"[2] to appoint the implacable Commissioner Lin with full powers to put an absolute stop to the opium trade. His

---

1. *As 1840 progressed, Chinese irritation grew, and the government of Kwangtung offered the following rewards:*

For the capture of Elliot, Morrison or Bremer,	*50,000 dollars each.*
For their heads, each	*30,000 dollars*
For the British officer, each	*10,000 "*
For his head, each	*5,000 "*
For the capture of a ship of the line	*100,000 "*
For "a three piecey-bamboo" – a three-masted	*25-50,000 "*
merchantman according to size.	

2. *From Maurice Collis' book "Foreign Mud."*

reputation as an honest administrator was well-known throughout the Flowery Land, and his nickname "Lin Ch'ing-t'ien meant "Lin, the Clear Sky" and was a most coveted title.

When Lin came to Canton, after being Governor of Kiangsu and Hu-Kuang Provinces, where he had become an expert on flood control, social relief, and tax collection etc. "He was 54, short and rather stout, with a keen dark eye looking out of a smooth, full round face, which except for a slender black beard, was hairless... he seldom smiled."[1]

Finally on 27th March 1839, 20,283 chests of opium were delivered up to Lin by Capt. Charles Elliot. "As the ships surrendered their opium it was broken up and mixed with water, salt and lime until it dissolved in trenches, then the liquid was made to flow through screens into a creek and from thence to the ocean."[2]

Wyndham continues:

> Large Tartar Forces are collecting throughout this vast Empire and the Edicts of the Emperor are fully as bombastic as ever. He orders his Generals not to spare us but to slay and destroy every one of us. He will find this no easy matter I reckon, and it is high time his pride should be brought down. Everyone who knows everything of these people concurs in thinking that Peking must be visited before he will accede to our terms.
>
> I have read every work I can get hold of concerning the Opium Question and have come to the conclusion that we have no right to date the present eruption to that cause, as we have been insulted, our Trade interfered with, and British subjects have been maltreated long before Opium was mentioned and we have only been too tardy in seeking redress.
>
> The vessels used for the importation of Opium into this country are termed clippers, from their being the fastest sailing vessels perhaps in existance. Three of them are lying within a few miles of this, they average from 120 to 300 tons burthen and from their build and equipment are very much like

1. *From "The Opium Clippers," by Basil Lubbock.*
2. *From "Commissioner Lin and the Opium War," by Hsin-pao Chang.*

what I should imagine the *Waterwitch*[1] to have been. A clipper will take this to Macao as they find a sale up there for their goods, and when war is declared they will prove very useful in taking letters up the coast. There are about 15 of them in these seas, with a cargo worth perhaps four millions amongst them which will be a severe loss to their owners, but the trade in this contraband article (opium) has long been a complete lottery.

"Opium Clippers were built for speed as the coast trade had its dangers. The China Seas had long been notorious for their pirates and clippers had to be heavily armed; there was no help from the British or "Celestial Navies" as the Chinese pirates hunted in swarms. In 1807 their fleet is said to have numbered between 500 and 600 sail. Later, at the height of their power, the pirate chiefs fell to quarrelling amongst themselves, and the Chinese Viceroy was able to treat with individual chiefs, so that you had ex-pirates serving in the Imperial Navy, helping to track down and capture their late fellow pirates.[1]" (Good prizes were offered!)

Persons guilty of piracy on the high seas were condemned by the Chinese penal code to be beheaded and their heads exhibited as a public spectacle. If the pirates resisted capture by government officers, a lingering death awaited them.

Wyndham continues:

The latitude of this place is decided to be 30 North and the dip of the Needle is quite extraordinary, fancy 43 in this low latitude! At the North Pole it is very little more. We know not how to account for this like many other wonders connected with the loadstone[2], which have puzzled the scientific.

1. *From "British Admirals & Chinese Pirates," by Grace Fox.*
2. *He is talking about the loadstone, the forerunner of the magnetic compass, to which "angle of dip" refers.*

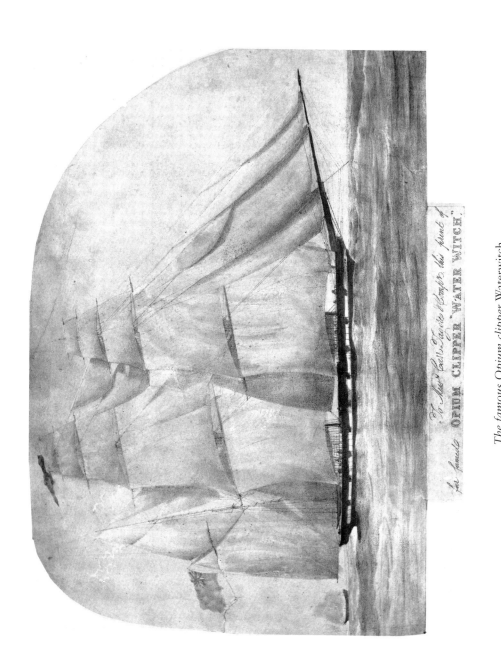

The famous Opium clipper Waterwitch.
By Courtesy of the National Maritime Museum, Greenwich.

The *Waterwitch*

From the "Mariner's Mirror," we learn that the *Waterwitch* was 92 tons, built at Kidderpore in 1831, owner Dent. She was known as the *Flying Waterwitch* and was quite famous in her day. These clippers were taking contraband goods, so it was essential that they should be built for speed, and although not so large as some of the big tea clippers, she was very fast for her size. Her first owners were merchants of Calcutta and by 1848 all the shares were in the names of Lancelot and John Dent. We hear that the *Waterwitch* was amongst the clippers attempting the passage to China in the unfavourable monsoon.

In 1833 the *Waterwitch* is listed as making two trips in the year between Calcutta and Lintin. In 1835 she is mentioned as being the first away to Canton after the sales of opium in Calcutta in January.

In 1836 we hear that the crack clipper *Waterwitch* had a rough time meeting a typhoon on her outward passage and a cyclone on the way home between Singapore and Calcutta; her valiant crew had to cut away her main and mizen masts, at which the gallant little ship righted herself, and finally reached Lintin, with neither her hull or her cargo damaged. In 1838 the *Waterwitch* did the trip from China to Calcutta in the winter in 25 days, and in June and July 43 days, in fact she was the fastest – the heroine of her year!

Island of Chusan,
November 1st, 1840

To his mother,

We have at least been obliged to quit our encampment in consequence of the tents being no longer able to keep out the cold and rain, and have therefore all moved into the few remaining huts on the beach, which formerly composed the suburbs of the principal town on this island. Glass for the windows is almost unknown so we are obliged to be content with a bag of paper for a substitute. This is wet weather and is soon destroyed and the cold north wind blows through every opening. I have been contemplating a trip to England in consequence of severe attacks of dysentry[1], fever, and ague in quick succession, leaving me in a most wretched condition and quite unfit for the active duties of my profession. However, thank goodness the last fortnight has completely restored me.

Many of the fellow sufferers in the Troops have been recommended a change of climate, and Manilla and the Phillipine Islands have been mentioned.

The Troops, I am sorry to say, are in the most pitiful condition and we are losing men at a much faster rate than we did in the notoriously unhealthy campaign of Rangoon. One Regiment, the Cameronians (26th), have alone buried 82 men during the last month. We have hitherto been exceedingly fortunate, but are now beginning to lose men in the same proportions as our neighbours, and though every attention is paid them and no expense spared in procuring them nutritious food, yet they will not rally poor fellows! and I fear many of them are destined to leave their bones in this horrible place.

The Chinese have brought us of late presents of cattle and poultry, and their whole demeanour towards us seems peaceable; still they will not give us up Anstruther[2] or the other prisoners they have in their possession. We have received intelligence of Anstruther being treated exceedingly well by them, which is so far satisfactory, but still we think the Admiral should insist on his restoration before he goes down to Canton to negotiate and be humbugged.

However this Expedition may turn out, unless we show more determination than we have hitherto done, the Chinese will oblige us to go over the same ground again before many years are over. The Admiral, we understand, was ordered by the Government to refrain if possible from warfare, and I dare say he is not so much to blame as his superiors, though possibly all the odium will be thrown on his shoulders should he fail.

---

1. From "*The Royal Naval History of the War*" we hear that between July 13th and Dec. 31st, 1840, at Chusan, there were 5,329 admissions to hospital and 448 deaths amongst Europeans alone.
2. There is an interesting paragraph on Anstruther in Clagette Blake's book about "*Charles Elliot R.N.*", which says: "Capt. Elliot was alarmed at the Chinese capture and mistreatment of Capt. Anstruther of the Madras Artillery, Lt. Douglas R.N., Commander of the brig Kite, and several other survivors from the Kite including Mrs. Noble, wife of the sailing master. These individuals had been loaded with heavy leg-irons and forced into tiny cages which were exposed in the market-places of towns in the island." The prisoners were finally released and brought south by the British Troops evacuating Ting-hai in March; it also shows how skippers took their wives aboard on long voyages!

Chusan, Dec. 23rd, 1840.

During the last few days the thermometer has generally been below freezing point, which we find by no means agreeable in our very dilapidated tenements. However, we have all recovered our health and spirits and are able to take long walks into the interior without fear of being molested.

Our native spies are daily bringing us reports of the raising of Troops on the mainland, and those long acquainted with these people declare affairs will not be finally settled without a deal more bloodshed.

The Chinese are bringing in all kinds of curiosities and I could spend any number of dollars if I had them in my possession. Some of the porcelain is very fine but they ask exorbitant prices. We are burning candles made of vegetable tallow which grows very abundantly on the trees here; the tallow is extracted from a kind of berry and answers the purpose famously. There is an immense demand for opium all along the coast and the Opium Clippers are reaping an excellent harvest. Some of them are selling the drug at 1,150[1] Dollars the chest, which is about five times its prime cost in India, so you may judge what fortunes are now being made, when some Merchants[2] have four or five of these ships entirely employed in the trade.

We have established a little Club where we go and gather all the scandal and news that's stirring, and in the evening go there for a quiet rubber of whist, but we miss ladies' society very much and no other can compensate for the loss.

I suppose you will be thinking of me at your family party Xmas Day, and I dare say if drinking of health is of any use I shall be in the enjoyment of it. I have an old friend, a Major of the Queen's[3] 49th coming to dine with me that day.

The Chinese are the most expert thieves and hardly a day passes without someone suffering by it. When the crime is proved against them they get a good flogging and have their tails cut off close to their heads, so we're always able to pick out the bad characters afterwards, and, at the same time, it is a great punishment to them; as I believe they would any day rather loose a finger than "a tail." (*A pigtail. Ed.*)

---

1. *The dollar before 1860 was the Spanish Carolus dollar with an intrinsic value of 4/2d., and an exchange value in China ranging from 4/6d. upward. –From "Far Eastern International Relations," by Morse and MacNair.*
2. *Merchants such as Lancelot Dent and Jardine & Matheson, reckoned to make £20 a chest of opium, and as they handled 6,000 chests p.a. in the 1830s, their income was about £120,000 then; it increased later.*
3. *49th (The Hertfordshire) Regiment of Foot which became "The Royal Berkshire Regiment."*

From Hsin-pao Chang's book

"Commissioner Lin and the Opium War"
P. 13. "The Challenge to the Old Order."

"The differences in culture and institutions, the problem of diplomatic equality, and the conflicts over judicial sovereignty would not have resulted in war had Sino-British contacts not increased so greatly. The Industrial Revolution predetermined the vast British commercial expansion, which brought traders with growing frequency and persistence to China's shores. The East India Company had performed its historical function, and by the turn of the century it had become conservative and chary of new demands and reform. It was left behind in the age of the new mercantilism and eventually lost its monopoly. The chief role in the nineteenth-century British overseas expansion was taken over by the private traders, who began to appear in Canton as early as the late 1760s.

"The early private English firms in China were well known as "agency houses." Up to the 1820s, their job was selling and buying for firms mainly in London and India on commission, but eventually many houses took on some "speculation," especially in opium and rice, on their own account. Thus in the 1830s, Jardine, Matheson and Company, the most influential of the private firms, was trading successfully in these articles while also performing agency activities.

"William Jardine (1784–1843) joined Magniac and Company in 1825 after spending fifteen years as a company ship's surgeon and several years in Canton as a resident agent. By 1820 he had become Danish Consul in Canton and was soon trading with Manila and Singapore. A few years later he joined Magniac, which was under the charge of Jardine. In 1832 the firm took on the name, Jardine, Matheson and Company.

"Operating mainly with outside funds, the agency business required only a very modest amount of capital. With the decline of the East India Company, the private firms grew both in number and importance. By 1834 they were handling more than half of Britain's trade with China. They were indeed vanguards of the nineteenth-century British Empire, funneling the resources of underdeveloped areas into its economic system and seeking new markets all over the world for its surplus industry. This rapid expansion almost immediately clashed with China's containment policy. Under the old Canton system, built on the doctrine that the "Celestial Empire does not value things brought from a distance," there was no room for more trade."

Chinese government officials did not offer protection or assistance to trade. Instead, they drained it with ruinous rapacity. They exacted 100,000 taels from the Hong merchants in 1832 to finance the campaign against the Lien-chou's insurrection, and 120,000 taels in 1833 for public relief. Besides these emergency collections, the Hong merchants paid out annual presents and contributions which in 1834, for example, amounted to 456,000 taels, breaking down as follows.

Tribute to the Emperor	55,000 taels
Repairs along the Yellow River	30,000 "
Expenses of an agent at Peking	21,600 "
Birthday presents to the Emperor	130,000 "
Similar presents to the hoppo	20,000 "
Presents to the hoppo's mother or wife	20,000 "
Annual presents to various officers	40,000 "
Compulsory purchases of native ginseng	140,000 "
	456,000 taels

The Hong merchants, entrusted with the management of the foreign community, were totally uninterested and incompetent in public affairs. They had the monopoly over foreign trade but lacked sufficient capital for large dealings. Although there was an official regulation forbidding them from going into debt with foreigners, the temptation was irresistible. They paid an interest of 1.5 percent a month, and the prospect of lending money at this high rate was what attracted the first private English traders to Canton in the 1770s. In the 1830s the annual Hong debts due foreigners were usually in excess of 3 million dollars, and we read much about the bankruptcies of the Hong merchants. Their position was so precarious that Beale and Company made it clear to its constituents that its "Agents in

Canton are not responsible for the failure of Hong Merchants, to whom they may have disposed of goods on account of their constituents, as a commission of 3% cannot be considered likewise a premium against bad debts."

Britain's economy was undergoing a great change, and British traders to China accordingly adopted a new outlook. But the Chinese refused to make any adjustment. After 1834 Britain opened her trade to all, but China clung to the monopoly of the Hong merchants. The economic force behind the free traders was too great to be restricted or contained. They had a mission: to tear down the inadequate Canton system and to rebel against the outmoded tribute diplomacy.

In the broad sense, the Opium War was a clash between two cultures. One was agricultural, Confucian and stagnant, and in the quicksand of a declining dynastic cycle. The Taiping rebellion was only a decade away, and the disintegrating economic, political, and social factors were already at work. The other society was industrial, capitalistic, progressive, and restless. When the two met, conflicts were inevitable, and the defeat of China was equally inevitable.

But the vital force that brought on the cultural conflict was Britain's commercial expansion. The friction that arose in the realms of diplomacy, law, and government was merely symptomatic of the basic problem – expansion versus containment. The opium trade was an indispensable vehicle for facilitating this expansion and the two could not be separated. Had there been an effective alternative to opium, say molasses or rice, the conflict might have been called the Molasses War or the Rice War. The only difference would have been a matter of time: in the hypothetical case, the major article of import being harmless, the lethargic Chinese would not have been alarmed into action so soon. The war could have been postponed, but not avoided.

Wyndham goes on: "We have established a little Club where we go and gather all the scandal and news that's stirring, and in the evening go there for a quiet rubber of whist, but we miss ladies' society very much and nothing can compensate for the loss.

I suppose you will be thinking of me at your family party Xmas Day, and I dare say if drinking of health is of any use I shall be in the enjoyment of it. I have an old freind, a Major of the Queen's 49th coming to dine with me that day.

While Wyndham was at Chusan, negotiation between Capt. Elliot and the Chinese Commissioner Keeshen dragged on until the end of the year. Elliot in *Wellesley*, lay at Linton, near the Forts of Chuenpee and the Bogue which were almost daily strengthened. The Expeditionary Force, also at this time was increased, notably by the arrival of seven Companies of the 7th Madras Infantry and the Honourable East India Company's iron steamer *Nemesis*, Master William Hutcheson Hall, R.N., "a vessel" says Ouchterlony, "destined to be very conspicuous in all the most important achievements of the War." From the Royal Naval History of the War.

The *Nemesis* was known to the Chinese as the devil ship and the *Nevermiss* among the British tars.

Wyndham was still on Chusan Island on January 20th, 1841, when he wrote: "I am ordered on a short expedition into the interior of the island to reconnoitre the country. I suppose we shall be away about a week and I rather look forward to it, as anything is better than the dull monotony of this place, only it is cold to allow of a bivouac being agreeable.

"We have established a regular correspondence with the prisoners at Ningpo by means of a spy. Anstruther's narrative of his capture and treatment since is most interesting. We have always been accustomed hitherto to look upon the Chinese as more civilized than any other Eastern nation, but their behaviour to their prisoners is more barbarous than anything you can possibly suppose. Poor Anstruther was put in a cage three feet high, three feet long and two feet wide, with heavy chains for his ankles, wrists and neck and left in this way for four weeks. He is a very stout man so you can imagine the misery he has endured. However, I think nothing of his sufferings to those of his fellow captives. Mrs. Noble, a lady by birth and education, was wrecked in her husband's ship off the coast and taken prisoner by the Chinese; her husband and infant perished in the wreck before she was taken, and these brutes have treated her exactly the same as Anstruther except that her irons were not quite so heavy.

Nemesis attacking Junks.

By kind permission of the National Maritime Museum, Greenwich.

In addition to her other miseries she was near her confinement. My feelings towards these people since the above account reached me are considerably changed and if we are ever doomed to meet in the field I'll engage that they will meet with very little pity from our Troops."

Wyndham Baker writing on board the Transport *Eagle*, at Hong-kong, on June 26th, 1841, said they moved up to Canton about the middle of March when they took the Factories.[1]

Wyndham continues his letter of June 26th, 1841, saying that Elliot, having a positive prohibition from home not to destroy the town of Canton, concluded a patched-up kind of Treaty with the Viceroy, and made a virtue of necessity by telling them their town was safe on condition they opened the trades. To this the Mandarins consented, and the trade was going on briskly till about the 12th of May, when it was understood that the Chinese had collected 70,000 Tartar Troops in or near Canton, that the Merchants' lives were threatened and trade was at a standstill. About six weeks previous to this, Sir G. Bremer had started from Calcutta to bring reinforcements. Wyndham says: "I was at this time in command of a small Detachment of Artillery on an Island which was the key to the River, being at its narrowest part, when the relieving Squadron passed my Island almost within hail but were unable to take me along much to my disgust.

"The Chinese behaved much better than was expected of them. They found their town was in a very awkward position from the fire of the shipping on one side and the Troops surrounding it on the other, and soon came out to offer a ransom of 6,000,000 Dollars for the City, a sum equal to about 1½ millions sterling."

Hunter in his "Fan Kwae at Canton" declares that a licence paid to Peking by a Hong merchant could amount to as much as £55,000 sterling; while Basil Lubbock tells us that in 1841, when the burden of ransoming Canton from the troops of Sir Hugh Gough, fell chiefly upon the Hong merchants, Howqua, the chief merchant, gave 1,100,000 dollars, Pwankeiqua 260,000; and the rest of the Co-hong 640,000 dollars. He also says that this was not the only time poor

1.   *See Further Information: page 155 The Hong Merchants, the Factories and Pidgin-English*

Howqua[1] paid out a million. However, we hear, that in spite of all this, when he valued his fortune in 1834, it was 26 million dollars, about five million odd sterling – quite a considerable fortune in those days. Howqua was by far the greatest of the Hong merchants and was renowned for his kindness to foreigners, for on several occasions he let them off their debts. He lived extremely frugally in spite of his immense wealth, and his portrait shows a thin, frail, ascetic rather pinched little face with thoughtful eyes and a pointed beard.

Wyndham says: "The ransom was accepted and after 10 days of excessive labour and fatigue they returned on board ship and my Detachment was also taken on board, so we are now waiting here for the steamers and Troops coming on.

"Sir G. Bremer has already arrived by steamer but what his plans are no one knows. The Emperor's Edicts get more amusing daily as he does not believe his brave Tartar Troops can be beaten.

"We have now been upwards of a year in China and instead of progressing have rather gone backwards. Then the whole line of coast was in a defenceless condition, now it is all fortified. Their gunnery is considerably improved and they are by no means deficient in courage; as we found when we captured some of their heavy guns, with such names as: 'Tamer of Barbarians,' 'Scourge of Foreigners,' etc.

"The ransom money or a part of it is to be given as Prize Money and the most sanguine tell me that I shall get £1,500 by it. The Kurnoul business which I flattered myself would bring in about £500, has as yet only given me £50. [*Their big gun is now in the R.M.A. grounds. – Editor.*]

"I am now looking forward to our second trip to the north as I had quite enough hardship[2] at Chusan. I have been lately staying with my old friend Baldwin at Macao and was there able to replenish my wardrobe which was in a most woeful condition. The Merchants there live in the most splendid style imaginable, these fellows have their tables laid for 20 or 30 for breakfast and dinner, and if you put

1. *Howqua was painted by George Chinnery, an artist who sailed with the Navy and painted for them. Naval ships often carried artists in those days to record events, as likewise Army Cadets were encouraged to be draughtsmen – long before the days of photography. – Editor.*
2. *Basil Lubbock in his account of the taking of Canton, tells us that disease played havoc with the men, dysentry, ague and fever, being the most prevalent.*

Howqua *painted by George Chinnery who sailed with the Navy 1774–1852. Senior Hong Merchant at Canton, China c.1831, a great friend to British Officers dealing with Chinese merchants. By Courtesy of the Trustees of the Tate Gallery*

up with them for a month they would press you to stay for another on going away, and are quite annoyed if you do not ask your friends to the house as you would in an hotel. Such hospitality I never saw before.

"It is quite extraordinary to trace the fatality which has followed us from the commencement of this business. Sir F. Maitland was first selected to take charge of it, but his death took place 'ere he received the appointment from England. General Oylander died on our passage to Chusan and we had great losses at that hateful place. There was the loss of the *Golcondah* with 300 Troops on board; the accident to the *Melville* which obliged the Admiral to leave her behind on the campaign; also the sickness of Admiral Elliot which obliged him to return to England leaving the whole management in the hands of that imbecile fellow Captain Elliot.

"At Peking and the country around we are looked upon as pirates and, knowing our inability to bring vessels any way up the river, they have only to burn everything in front and we must give it up through lack of provisions alone. The transport of artillery and the necessary heavy stores, without cattle, is a work of extreme difficulty and a mile a day would be capital work. Again, the whole of our rear must be kept open all the way up from the mouth of the Peiho, a line of 760 miles. It has become much the fashion in England to laugh at the Chinese soldiers, but before this war is brought to a conclusion their characters will have gone a great change. At sea they never can cope with us, but on land, where they have such odds in their favour as regards numbers, I think we yet might be taught a lesson, though we have decided advantages over them in gunners.

"I believe the Tea Trade[1] is quite at an end, so you had better lay in a large supply in case the war is not terminated for a long while. When thrashed the Chinese inform the Emperor that they have been victorious, and until he knows the rights of the case little can be expected of him. The old wretch must have led a pleasant life of it, as no unpleasant truth is ever allowed to reach his ear if they can avoid

1. *There was a 200% duty on tea so there was smuggling in the tea trade as well as in the opium trade; each year fast clippers from Britain, Europe and America, lay ready at the port of Canton, to load the first of the new seasons' teas, and be first in the great race home to British ports*

it. The only honest man[1] we have had to deal with, told the truth and had his lands confiscated and his life threatened. However, the Emperor cannot be much longer kept in ignorance, as cannon balls will soon be flying over his palace at Peking unless he comes to terms.

"Amongst our other disasters consequent on the last typhoon, we lost all our gun carriages which could not be replaced nearer than India, but luckily we recovered them all by divers, though they had gone down in water three fathoms deep."

---

1. *Commissioner Lin.*

Typhoon at Hong Kong

J.R. Baldwin's Esq.,
Macao, Monday morning.
July 26th, 1841.

To his Mother and Sisters,

We are anticipating a speedy move to the northward, but for some reason best known to the Commander-in-Chief we are still stationary at Hongkong, so I have applied for a week's leave before commencing another campaign to the unpropitious north. Accordingly I came over here on the 14th and after spending a very pleasant week with my old friend Baldwin, I availed myself on the 21st, of H.M.'s Schooner *Hebe*, which the old Commodore had kindly given up for the accommodation of the officers returning to Hongkong. She is a nice little vessel of 45 tons and as we started with a fair wind and fine weather we hoped to reach our destination (a distance of only 40 miles) that evening or the following morning. H.M.'s Cutter *Louisa* started at the same time with the Commodore Elliot and staff and though crowded ourselves we still anticipated a nice little trip.

We had hardly made above 15 miles when a most deceitful calm came on and we were obliged to drop anchor for the night. At midnight the sea became much disturbed with a fresh breeze blowing which rapidly increased to a gale, and by morning a most fearful typhoon broke on us with all its force.

You must have often read and heard of these hurricanes, but I defy any description to equal the reality. I have encountered several severe gales before now, but never did I ever witness anything half so terrific as this. Still I did not apprehend any serious danger as we were in a tight little sea trap with plenty of hands and several old and experienced Naval Officers on board to help us. However I soon became aware that we were in a most perilous situation and by 10 a.m. every man on board believed his last moments were numbered.

Both anchors with all the cable on board had been run out but notwithstanding this we drifted before the wind as if we were under canvas, with the sea making a clear breach over our little craft. It was just at this time that a wave struck her so violently that she healed over on her beam and it was with the utmost risk that they succeeded in cutting away the masts. She righted a little, but was wholly unmanageable and continued drifting; imagine our horror at catching a glimpse through the mist of a rocky point within 100 yards of us, towards which we were seeping bodily at a fearful velocity. We were now within 50 yards and could see the surf beating on the rocks 10 times worse than at Madras, and the natives were down on the beach waiting to seize on our wreck which appeared inevitable as we knew these people to be pirates of the worst kind, and how little mercy we had to expect from them should any of us by any possibility have reached the shore.

As for myself I determined on perishing with the vessel and should have foundered with her in preference to being murdered by these wretches. Others more tenacious of life had stripped with the vain hope of swimming to shore – I say vain as we have all since agreed that no one could have crossed the rocks without being dashed to pieces. One and all looked the picture of despair but not a groan or a murmur was uttered, as we silently waited our certain doom. A minute elapsed and Lt. Collinson R.N. (as brave and fine a fellow as ever lived) who had taken charge of the craft from the commencement of the storm said: "the current is taking us clear," and it was at once apparent to everyone that we had escaped the most fearful danger.

We really had the most miraculous escape from the Typhoon. Never to the last moment of my existence shall I forget the joy of that minute, it seemed as if I had taken a fresh lease of life. In five minutes we had cleared the last point and were drifting out to sea when Providence still befriended us and the anchor almost hitherto useless brought us up. I have in my short career been placed in many trying situations and gone through some perils and dangers, but never was I or anyone else on board so near the end as we were on this awful occasion. The feelings I had then are of course difficult to describe, but of course gratitude to God for my escape was uppermost. We rode pretty securely through the remainder of the gale and the following morning at 8 o'clock it had so much abated that we one and all set to work to make Jury Masts and that night arrived safely at Macao, without having had a stick of dry clothes or anything to eat and drink besides biscuit and water, since the storm commenced. At Macao we were almost looked upon as ghosts, as no one ever imagined we should live out the storm. The destruction here has been very great, but at Hongkong, which is supposed to be the most secure harbour, it has been dreadful, more than 30 ships injured more or less and some totally lost.

The poor old Commodore in the *Louisa* was wrecked within a few miles of us when we were in that perilous situation, but luckily for them they got into a sheltered little bay where they were able to swim ashore. The natives behaved very badly to them, knocked down the poor old man, and would have taken their lives had it not been for someone who spoke a little English who said he would give them their lives for £300, which of course was gladly accepted. They were accordingly brought over here in a Chinese boat to get the ransom. They landed here in a most woeful plight, without anything but their trousers on, but it was very fortunate for them that they were not known as they would have been sent to Peking, or perhaps killed for the reward put on their heads. They were almost discovered as a bit of the Commodore's epaulettes floated on shore with his orders etc. which the Chinese declared must belong to a Mandarin, and they had some difficulty in persuading them that they were only peaceful merchants.

Everyone from the *Hebe* was ill after this, but I escaped with a slight attack of fever and the loss of some of my clothes, however it will be long 'ere I forget the 21st of July.

We hear of there being a considerable addition to our Corps immediately, which will promote me to a Lieutenancy. The difference in pay is very trifling not being more than £60 per annum, which will make my income a little more than £300 a year, which is more than I deserve.

On our northern trip we take on at a rough guess about 2,500 Bayonets and the Marines from the Men-of-War will make it up to nearly 3,000. The remainder stay here to garrison this Island, all of them sickly.

The *Conway*, which I was so long on board, has just returned to England with the invalids of the Navy and the wounded. They like-wise take home a little more than 2¼ millions of the Canton Ransom money, so I dare say the Whigs will be inclined to make a good deal of her when she arrives. The silver she had on board weighed upwards of 55 tons.

I am longing to hear something about Isabella's marriage[1] which will be quite an old story by the time this reaches you.

Believe me,

Yours most affectionately,

Wyndham Baker.

---

1. *I am tempted to put in this note about his sister Isabella Octavia Baker, as she was my great-grandmother. She married the Revd Peter Bellinger Brodie, Rector of Rowington, Warwickshire; who was afterwards celebrated for his collections of fossilized wood-lice (Archaeoniscus Brodiei – called after him) and fossil insects, now in the Natural History Museum. His grand-daughter Gladwys Wyndham Sanders (my mother), used to carry his hammer when a little girl, so I inherited his fossil cabinet.*

Extracts from a letter of Wyndham's written from:

Hongkong, Canton River,
August 21st, 1841.

After lying inactive and dying of ennui for the last two months we are once more all bustle and activity, in consequence of the arrival of the new Admiral Sir W. Parker[1] and the new Plenipotentiary, Sir H. Pottinger.[2] They only arrived two days ago having made the shortest passage between England and China ever heard of being a little over two months!

Sir H. Pottinger proceeds to Canton today and will state the lowest possible terms he will accept and at once declare war against China. We shall proceed with all possible dispatch to the northward to Amoy, where we have already been twice insulted, this is to the first place we attack; from there to Ningpo, and again take up our winter quarters at horrid Chusan. Whether Sir H. Pottinger adheres to the plans of his predecessor remains to be seen, some think he will make a dash at the capital, but in our crippled state, 3,000 all included, it would be weak beyond measure.

The Chinese are a most strange deceitful lot to deal with, only this week they gave us six millions to leave Canton and promised not to meddle any further; now we have just found them blocking the river up with a regular breakwater of huge masses of granite which would have stopped any vessels passing up. This was almost completed when they were interrupted by our steamer who instantly made them knock off, and she is still up there making them remove every stone of it before she leaves.

It is fortunate we have got clear of Elliot as the Chinese have long known how to deal with him, I don't think the new Plenip. will listen to their humbug.

The expenses of this Expedition are most enormous and will rather astonish the House when the account is produced, the expense of the Transports alone cost more than the sum voted by Parliament, viz. £400,000.

It has now been decided that the Island of Hongkong shall be ceded to us

1. *Afterwards Admiral-of-the-Fleet Sir William Parker, G.C.B. Had been one of Nelson's Captains. Appointed C.-in-C. China May, 1841. After six years as a Lord of the Admiralty became C.-in-C. Med. A renowned disciplinarian.*
2. *Sir Henry Pottinger Bt., G.C.B. Soldier, diplomatist, and a 'resolute man.' Sent out by Lord Palmerston to relieve Charles Elliot. Became first Governor of Hongkong.*

These notes made by Mr. Blackwood of Edinburgh.

forever as a trading depot and that on our evacuating Chusan our prisoners will be delivered over to us; application was at the same time made for a Company of Artillery and a Regiment to garrison Hong-kong. This duty fell to our Company and we were immediately packed off on board the *Conway*[1] and away we sailed for Hong-kong. On our arrival there after a pleasant little voyage we found the place deserted and instead of affairs being settled it looked more warlike than ever. We crammed on all sail and joined the Fleet off Whampoa below Canton; we found there lots of employment in making Forts and Batteries on either side of the river. The Chinese must have lost 5,000 men since this business broke out; the remnants of their scattered troops have taken shelter in Canton, and as the Plenip. had positive orders from England not to destroy this place we were obliged to rest on our oars, hoping in the interim the Emperor would see the folly of resisting us longer. After lots of threats the Mandarins at Canton consented to trade with us, about 40 merchant vessels have gone up and are filling rapidly with tea, so you will have no reason to complain of a shortage in that commodity.

I was disappointed in the Factories in Canton but it must have been an enormously wealthy place, and they say that if we had destroyed it, the people would never again have had any confidence in us, so it was fortunate we spared the town. We have taken upwards of 1,200 guns, some of English manufacture and most of them superior to those taken at Chusan. The Last Edict from the Emperor was most warlike, he declared that he would fight it out, determined that either England or China should perish in the attempt as he knew that the world was not large enough for two such forces at the same time.

---

[1] *Capt. E. Hewitt R.D., R.N.R., (Retd.) of the HMS Conway, Merchant Navy Cadet School, Llanfairpwyll, Anglesey, has kindly sent me the following note on the various* Conways, *from* "The Story of the Conways".

"*Wyndham Baker served in a frigate* HMS Conway *of which both I and John Masefield have prints. Soon after she returned from the China Station she was loaned to a Committee of gentlemen in Liverpool and became the first residential training ship for officers hoping to join the Merchant Navy. A few years later she was found to be too small and was replaced by HMS* Winchester, *the ships exchanging names and this ship in turn was too small and was replaced by HMS* Nile *in 1875;* Nile *had also taken the name of* Conway *and this is the one in which your Uncle was trained and about which he wrote, not only the books you refer to, but also two histories published by Heinemann under the title 'HMS* Conway,' *as well as a novel 'New Chum.'*

"*In 1953 the third wooden wall ex* Nile *then* Conway *was wrecked in the Menai Strait while going for a re-fit and we have just commissioned the new stone frigate carrying her name.*"

Amoy

Transport *Palmyra*,
Amoy Harbour, Sept. 3rd, 1841.
Via Falmouth overland.

To his mother and sister,

After numerous changes and a week of bustle and preparation, we were at last enabled to put to sea on the evening of the 21st, leaving behind a garrison of somewhat more than 1,200 men and some small Men-of-War to keep Her Majesty's new possessions of Hong-kong, during our absence. Our Fleet consisted of 14 Men-of-War including four steamers convoying some 30 Transports with Troops and provisions, and you can hardly imagine a much prettier scene than when we were all getting under weigh together. I had been looking forward to a very pleasant little voyage after being cramped up in that delectable place Hong-kong. Fresh air alone was a rarity as there we seldom had anything between a calm and a gale, in consequence of the place being surrounded by high barren hills intercepting every breeze; in this I was disappointed as I was quite an invalid all the way up owing to an attack of influenza which I believe I should still be teased with had it not been for the excitement of the attack on the 26th.

The bad sailing of some of the Transport detained us considerably so we did not sight the land marking the entrance to the harbour till the afternoon of the 25th. We had the advantage of a fine commanding breeze and the Men-of-War at once dashed through the entrance, which is so narrow that the Batteries completely command the passage. We observed several men and soldiers on the Batteries but they only fired a few random shots at us as we ran through, and they fell perfectly harmless.

It being dark when we came to an anchor that evening, little idea could be formed of the extent of the fortifications which were nearly five and a half miles distant, and as little was known about the place, every hero had his own notion and was quite sure that the General[1] and the Admiral[2] must conclude by following the only course that common sense pointed out, and thus having satisfied himself retired to bed full of hope for the morrow.

---

1. *Sir Hugh Gough, later Field-Marshal & Viscount. In command at Canton in March 1841 and throughout the rest of the campaign. Became C.-in-C. India in 1843.*
2. *Admiral Sir William Parker.*

Showing the Queen & Blenheim at Amoy, August 26th, 1841.
By kind permission of the National Maritime Museum, Greenwich.

At dawn each day every telescope was at work examining the surrounding land which positively appeared studded with Batteries looking most formidable, and as we know that these people are celebrated throughout China as the boldest and the best soldiers, we calculated on a stout resistance, particularly as they had gained considerable confidence in driving away the *Alligator* with another Man-of-War some time before. The Admiral, General and the Heads of Departments soon after embarked in a steamer for the purpose of running in near the Batteries to sound the depth of water and make a general reconnaisance. They went quite close in under the heaviest Batteries without being molested, so fully did the Chinese think us in their power, that they did not wish to disturb the steamer for fear of our making off in case they might loose what they believed to be within their grasp. It took some time to make the necessary arrangements for the attack so that no move took place amongst the Fleet till about 12 o'clock, when the two big steamers *Queen* and *Sesostris* ran alongside their long Battery and opened the Ball. The *Druid* and *Blonde* then moved down to silence the Batteries on the Island of Celonigson, and as we were ordered to follow their motions but keep out of gun shot, we ran in with them and thus had the best view of any ship of what was going forward as the line of battle ships took up their position and the firing was now general along the whole line. I am at a loss to give you a tolerable account of it, but the enemy had upwards of 400 guns employed against us – at all events you may form some opinion of the smoke and noise, but really it was a magnificent sight and I only wish I was a better hand with my brush to give you a tolerable idea of it on paper.

The Batteries were riveted with masonry upwards of nine feet thick and covered in front with turf, so as to render them splinter-proof. The ships, although within close range, were unable to make any impression and the Chinese returned shot for shot doing almost as much damage as we did them. About 2 o'clock we were following in the wake of the *Blonde* which by this time had come to anchor broadside on to the lower Battery; then we found the shot coming very close over us, so stood over to the opposite shore, where we soon found we had got from the frying pan into the fire as the shots were flying over us in every direction. So finding ourselves rather awkwardly situated we advised the Captain to go about as there was no choice left us, so we anchored near the *Blonde* where there was a prospect of our services being soon required to land and take the Island of Celonigson. We had just got into the situation desired when the wind failed and we ran bang into the *Druid*, and amidst the confusion and smoke we were as near as possible blown into the water by her fire, and we totally prevented the *Druid* returning a shot as we lay broadside on to her, between her and the Battery; this occurred about 3 o'clock, and the *Blonde,* seeing the predicament we were in, immediately gave orders for the Troops to land.

The Marines, 26th Regiment, and myself with two 12-Pounders, accordingly took to the boats and made the best of our way towards the Island. The Chinese, after firing two or three rounds of grape, abandoned their guns and sallied down to meet us; the ground near the landing place being rather precipitous they had a considerable advantage over us. However, the moment the Marines got a footing they were soon dispersed, leaving the greater portion of their number dead on the ground. At half-past three the British Flag was flying from the summit of the Battery, three hours after the first shot was fired.

The General and his part of the force had arranged to come in the light steamers and land on the flank of the Long Battery the moment the firing had somewhat abated, but it was some time before they could subdue the fire sufficiently to allow of the Troops landing. On examining the works since, we found that the Chinese were so exceedingly well protected from the fire, that I believe the ships might have blazed away till now without doing them any injury, and it was only landing the Troops that drove them from their guns at last. In my opinion the great crime committed was not landing the Troops much earlier in the day, as by taking these in rear of their Batteries no guns could be brought to bear on them, and very little loss of life is to be apprehended when bows and arrows with very uncouth matchlocks are opposed to *our good trusty muskets!*[1] As it was, the *Wellesley* alone expended 1,200 rounds of shot and shell and the other ships about the same in proportion, but their practice was by no means good and therefore the execution they did was comparatively trifling. On the General landing, and the main body of the Troops, the Chinese came down to oppose them after the same fashion as they did to us, and with the same success. It being by this time near dark, the General hesitated (being unacquainted with the nature of the ground) to move on the city till the following morning.

1. *Col. Appleby, the Director of the National Army Museum kindly asked Mr John F. Ware to send me the following note on muskets.*
'Previous to the 1840s, the main system of firing a musket was by flintlock. In this a flint was held between two jaws on a hammer. This was 'cocked' and when released by a trigger, hit a steel striker plate, creating sparks which ignited powder in a pan. In turn this fired the main charge through a touch hole.'
'After the 1840s, the Army used the percussion system where the musket was fired similarly to a child's cap pistol, i.e. the hammer hit a cap which exploded and fired the main charge.' 'Both muskets were accurate up to 200 yards.'

The Post occupied by our party was the point from which we were to shell the city the following morning, so we were busily employed till a late hour in dragging our implements of destruction into position, so that I was glad enough about midnight to wrap my martial cloak around me and throw myself on the sward for a little sleep, from which I was more than once disturbed by an occasional shot from our outlying picquets.

At early dawn the General advanced towards the city and coming suddenly on a walled place on the outskirts, which was unoccupied, they marched into it and took possession. This place proved to be the stronghold and keep, and it was at once evident that from this commanding position they could threaten the city in any way they liked. The General accordingly gave out that the place would be fired unless the sum of six million dollars was paid for its ransom, but in the panic of the day before, the whole of the respectable people of the town and high Mandarins had fled, so that no person was found to stipulate the terms. Since this there has been no fighting of any kind so completely have they been defeated. Their loss has been by no means great – two to three hundred killed at the utmost – and our's has been very insignificant, but I cannot give the numbers as I have not yet seen the return of casualties. The rigging and masts of the ships were a good deal knocked about in proportion to the loss of life, which is easily accounted for by the elevation the Chinese give their guns, always firing over everything in the same horizontal plane.

The population of the city cannot be far short of 300,000 and the inhabitants, if you can judge by their houses, must be exceedingly wealthy. They carry on a vast trade from home with Singapore. At Formosa and along the whole Eastern coast, some of their junks are laden with the most costly merchandise and if retained it would pay the whole expenses of the war. From its proximity to the sea districts and its excellent harbour I should think this would suit us in every way better than Hongkong. There was formerly a British Factory here but no traces of it are now to be discovered. The fall of the place must be a very severe blow to the Chinese Government and if it does not convince them of the folly of any longer refusing our demands, nothing will. They had sent all their best Generals and Mandarins here and bragged to their friends at Canton of our being afraid to visit them; when they found the day was lost, three of the principal Mandarins destroyed themselves in front of our Troops.

Since active operations concluded I have been busily employed destroying guns and fortifications and otherwise injuring the Chinese to the best of my ability. The Troops in the city have picked up a considerable quantity of plunder and some quantity of Sycee silver,[1] which I could do with too, but of course it would not really do for officers to set them a bad example, though I have seen the most splendid and elegant satin dresses in the possession of some of them.

Our Troops are to be totally withdrawn from the town but the Island of Celonigson is to continue in our possession to hold the city in check till they pay the ransom money. Some Men-of-War remain behind with them, and the remainder of us move, the moment the wind is favourable, still further to the north. I believe Nangpo is to be the next point of attack, taking Chusan afterwards as a wintering place, so we shall have three Chinese Islands in our keeping before the end of the year. This must be very humbling to the Emperor[2] and I hope and trust he will at once see the necessity of giving in to our terms as this Expedition has not much honour or profit to anyone.

1. *Sycee silver, little lumps of solid silver shaped like a chinese woman's bound feet.*
2. *The Emperor was known as the Tao Kuang Emperor which meant 'Glorious Rectitude'.*
   From Maurice Collis' book 'Foreign Mud'.

N. China Campaign, Macao, Chusan and Nanking

Ningpo-foo,
The second City of Chekiang.
October 31st, 1841.

To his Mother & Sisters,

We left Amoy on Sept. 4th and had to beat against a headwind. Then we encountered a strong current which nearly swept us on to an Island at the entrance of the harbour. It was only a few nights after this that we were sitting on the Poop talking over the likelihood of some accident occuring as the ships were all crowded together and on different tacks, when suddenly we were hailed by a voice quite close, desiring us to put down the helm, and to our dismay we saw an enormous 74 bearing directly down on us with all sail set. We did all we could to clear her and she shortened sail with all possible speed, but a collision was unavoidable. Of all disasters which we are subject to at sea I think none can be worse than that of being run down in the dark and swallowed up before you well know what to do. You must have often heard of ships running foul of each other and one or both sinking, in this case the Captain lost all presence of mind and said she would cut us in two amidships. We all bustled down between decks hoping they would somehow protect us when the masts fell; crash after crash followed each other, then the noise suddenly ceased and we rushed up to find the big ship was actually clear without having done us very much damage. It appeared that two large spars which we had flung outside saved us, as they received the force of the concussion and caused the *Blenheim* to recoil immediately from us.

A few days after this we had some bad weather and the Fleet separated. We were three or four days without seeing a sail, and when the wind moderated we ran into the nearest anchorage at a place called "Buffaloes' Nose". We found a few of the Fleet there and by the 28th all had re-assembled, the following day we stood into the outer anchorage of Chusan; prior to this the steamers had been reconnoitring the Works which had been thrown up during our absence and which they described as gigantic, considering all had been done in six months.

The General and Admiral completed their plan of attack on the 30th and a desultory fire was kept up on both sides. The right of the Chinese Battery was within 2,500 yards of our shipping behind a low wall, over which our masts were visible. Several of their shot fell very near us but with the exception of one which knocked out the muzzle of one of the *Blonde*'s guns, I do not think they struck another ship. The Navy replied with shell which seemed to harass them a good deal. Some slight works and entrenched camps up the hill were just within range of the *Wellesley*'s guns, and their practice was really beautiful, every shell telling and bursting right in the centre.

To an Artillery Officer, the night before an attack is invariably tedious as before he can rest satisfied, 50 boxes require to be minutely examined, besides which the guns have to be got out of the hold and put in boats ready for landing; on this occasion however they gave me entire charge of the Rocket Battery, so my work was soon over and I managed to get a good sound sleep.

By early dawn on the 1st October everybody was on the qui vive; the steamers ran close in shore and the boats pushed off for the nearest point to land. We anticipated no opposition at the landing place as all the Batteries were on the other side of the hill and our ships kept up a constant fire on them. At the moment of our boats pulling off for the shore not a Chinaman was visible, but by the time we reached the beach the whole hill was covered with soldiers who poured in a very galling fire on us. In the confusion of landing, the 55th Foot formed as speedily as possible and advanced to storm the hill. The air seemed full of missiles of different kinds, from the whistle of a bullet to the strange noise of a cannon ball, and what with the navy firing over our heads and the Chinese firing at our heads it was very exciting.

A soldier, evidently a Mandarin of the Party, took up his post on a high peak just within range of our muskets waving a red flag and encouraging his men. The ships by this time had slackened their fire fearing some accident might happen to the advancing party, but their patience was not proof against this man's impertinence and a few shots were directed at him, these ploughed up the ground all round and still he remained unharmed, then all at once he disappeared a round shot having taken him in the stomach which tore him positively to atoms; another then rushed forward nothing daunted by the fate of his predecessor and displayed the flag. I did not see what became of him as the 55th had closed with them by this time, but believe the greater part of his brave comrades perished with the bayonet. There were

15 men and one officer of the 55th killed in taking this hill; the officer, being Junior Ensign of the Regiment, was carrying the Royal Colours when he was shot dead.

I could recount numerous instances of individual bravery amongst the Chinese which came under my notice this day. I had just turned round to hasten my party with the Rockets when I felt a blow on my back, but on examination found only a hole in my trousers and picked up the bullet at my feet, this same bullet had made a hole in my orderley's cap, and as he was standing just behind me it probably saved my life. The General and several others this day were struck with spent balls.

At the top of the hill a magnificent scene was opened to me; in the valley below was a long Battery of some three miles in length crowded with soldiers, from this spot I opened with the Rockets with fair success but from my being so much elevated above them, they did not ricochet along the ground as much as I could have wished; whilst this was going on our guns went along the foot of the hill and opened in a heavy fire of grape and shell on the same point as ourselves which staggered them. The 18th Royal Irish now pushed on to drive them from the Battery and I was forced to cease firing. The moment they saw the 18th they took to flight, resembling a nest of ants beneath me, the whole valley seemed to move. All at once a Mandarin halted, a few joined him then more returned and in a few minutes 200 had rallied round him; with this chosen band he returned to the Battery apparently determined to defend his post to the last. They formed in tolerable order and advanced to meet the 18th who poured in a volley on them and charged; most of these brave fellows fell and their leader I afterwards saw amongst the slain and recognized from his gigantic stature, he was the second in command on the Island and a remarkably handsome man. The 18th continued their route along the Battery to storm the Citadel which was likely to offer a longer resistance. I soon rejoined the Guards Column with the Rifles and 55th who had overcome every obstacle along the ridge of the hill with little loss and were preparing to advance on the city. We, knowing the ground well, went by a path which took us to the top of the hill which completely commanded the City. A portion of the walls was soon cleared of its defenders and the storming party under cover of our guns climbed up the ladders, and in a few minutes more our flag was flying for the second time from the walls of Chusan. About the same time the 18th in the other direction had taken possession of the Citadel and the day was ours. By four o'clock that same afternoon we were once more located in the very buildings which had afforded us shelter last winter. Had we landed at the old place where the main body of the Chinese were waiting we should have had a bad time as they had 130 guns in position, as it was our losses throughout the day were something short of 50 men, but the Chinese were butchered to a fearful extent.

As before the Treasury had been sacked and all they left us was the Granary. The Chinese were fast advancing in the art of war, some of the brass guns we found here are beautifully cast and their only fault is that they do not put sufficient zinc in their gun-metal, and their carriages have been made very like ours, which they must have copied from last year. When it was thought we should keep possession of Chusan as a British Settlement, the Engineers planned a work to command the suburbs and town. During our absence the Chinese had built the Citadel on this ground and had certainly made a very strong position against all China with 200 men.

The more I see of these people the more extraordinary do I consider them. For instance, take the pith of two proclamations which we found side by side on the Walls. The first ordered that: "all respect should be paid to the grave of the barbarians who died here last year and that their ashes should be allowed to rest in peace." The other stated that: "the Barbarians had been driven away from Canton with great loss and that their leader one Bremer (Sir Gordon) had been taken and put to a lingering death, while his body was cut in pieces and his head still graces the Gate of Canton." We have ascertained that this was actually done to a poor sergeant of the 26th, who they obliged the populace to believe was the Commodore. The Chinese have more superstition than most people and they have a prophesy that in this year the present Emperor will be dethroned when ships come to China without sails, working against a dead head wind (of course by this they mean steamers), then they will fall under the government of a white woman coming from the far West.

From the 1st to the 7th, all the Artillery Officers were employed in destroying the Arsenals, powders etc., and collecting the brass guns for shipment of which there were 36; these will bring in about £4,000 to £5,000.

On the 8th we all embarked with the exception of 500 men who were left to garrison the Island during our absence. The Plenip. has published a Proclamation to the Chinese stating that we intend to hold this Island till the final settlement of affairs, so I suppose all the people will return to their homes. Chinhai was our next point of attack. The place was very highly fortified with a large force to defend it, being the key to Ningpo, and our most determined enemy U-Kiang resided there. This man was selected by the Emperor last year to go down and recover Chusan from us; just before he arrived we abandoned the place, after which he published the most bragging accounts of our having fled the moment he arrived. It was he who murdered poor Captain Stead whose head was found on a pole with an Englishman on either side of him. U-Kiang's clothes were made of tiger-skin and he had been known to partake of the blood of that animal. His last Edict was a curious production, he said he understood he had started for the north of Canton and that his only fear was that we should not dare come to Chinhai and he would loose the honour of capturing us, that a report prevailed that Amoy had fallen to our arms, but that it was a falsehood and anyone who circulated, thought, or dreamt it to be true, should lose his head. Ten days after this was published, Chinhai was in our possession and Mr. U-Kiang had poisoned himself.

On the 9th of October we landed two or three miles below the position of the enemy which looked most formidable. Next morning the ships of War engaged the Batteries and being with the Rockets I was able to keep up with the advancing columns. We soon drew near the right flank of the enemy who were drawn in large bodies on the hills in battle array. I commenced the Ball by trying a Rocket at them and they immediately opened every gun and wall piece at us. The Infantry divided into three columns and attacked them in three different points; the Chinese behaved with gallantry, but the British courage and discipline prevailed. In the course of an hour or so the Infantry had skirmished over the whole ground and the Chinese fled at all points towards the River, where the fugitives found themselves completely hemmed in and many drowned themselves in the River. The Chinese never had a more thorough defeat; the whole of the Public Records fell into our hands, besided upwards of 170 Pieces of Cannon (half of them brass), Arsenals etc., and the Chinese left Ningpo completely at our mercy, their whole force broken and dispersed. The whole country was so panic struck that had we advanced immediately we might have taken Nanking.

We embarked on the 13th and entered Ningpo without opposition. It is the second city in the Province, Hang-chow-foo being the metropolis. The population is about half a million, its walls enclose an area of about five miles and it lies in the centre of a very fertile and extensive valley, intersected in every direction by rivers and canals. The trade of this place must be very great owing to the number of large junks we found here, and the people appear exceedingly wealthy. After making a tour of the Walls on the 13th, we proceeded to this building which was the abode of the Mandarin who had Anstruther in custody last year. Our Mess Room was where he used to appear before the Mandarins and his prison cage was one of the great sights of the place. These buildings are so extensive that they accommodate ourselves, the Rifles and the Sappers – upwards of 500 with ease. The mob had entered the Palace before us and most of the valuables were moved, but in the Treasury we discovered 80,000 of Sycee Silver[1], and have seized besides several valuable junks .

Island of Chusan.
(N. China),
January 8th, 1842.

To his mother and sisters,

Since last I wrote to you from Ningpo at the beginning of November, I have only once had the pleasure of hearing from you, and as your letter had been some seven months on the road, being dated the end of April, I am in hopes every day, of receiving more recent intelligence, but fear some of your letters must have perished in the Steamer and Transport which have lately been wrecked in their passage hither.

I have been here for these last seven weeks in command of the Artillery at this Post. We have now pretty well got through the cold season which has been much more severe than it was last year. The long walks about the Island I have enjoyed exceedingly and it has made me stronger and healthier than I ever was before, but at the same time it has made me so stout that hardly any of my clothes will fit me, which at a place where it is impossible to replace them you may suppose is a great inconvenience and what I shall be reduced to bye and bye I can't think.

Nothing very particular as regards the Expedition has taken place since my last, but we hear of the Chinese assembling from every quarter and the Emperor is more furious than ever in his Edicts, and I think now it is beyond a doubt that before we bring affairs to a settlement we shall have to overthro' the present Dynasty and place one of our own creatures in his stead. How much it is to be regretted that our Home Authorities should have hampered

---

1. *This note on Sycee (silver) kindly sent to me by Miss Betsy W.D. Martin, M.A., of the Percival David Foundation of Chinese Art.*
    "The characters from which this word is derived mean pure silk (hsi ssu). Chinese lump silver is so called because, if pure, it may be drawn out under the application of heat into fine silk threads. Ingots of full quality which, incidentally, resembled a Chinese shoe in shape, were called Sycee."

us of for the want of Troops, here we are absolutely at a standstill from no other cause, when with the addition of 5,000 men at the commencement, we might have gone to Peking and been in possession of the old Tartar's person a year since; now it will take double that number to go up there and where they are to be drawn from it is difficult to say. We hear of a few arrivals but not a fiftieth part sufficient to meet the demand. The Governor General of India has promised to reinforce us with 5,000 or 6,000 men in the spring, that is if there is no probability of their being required on the Frontier. So here we are after two years dallying, actually beginning a war without the means at hand to carry it forward, for this of course we are in great measure indebted to the Whigs, and I only hope the Tories will at once see the necessity of adopting different plans or we shall never come to a finale.

The General burnt all the public buildings and arsenals and returned to Ningpo with his men none the better from their exposure in the cold and snow. He is now only waiting for the arrival of 200 or 300 more men to advance on the capital of the Province (Hang-chow-foo), where Lin of opium notoriety is stationed with 10,000 Troops.

A Chinaman whom we have long employed as a spy and the same person who conducted the correspondence last year has been kidnapped and put to death, together with some 30 shop-keepers at Ningpo, who opened their shops to us soon after our arrival, but they have not attempted to seize any Europeans since we returned here, though we know they have set high rewards on our heads.

This is a most beautiful Island and it is very likely after all that it will be kept in preference to Hongkong, notwithstanding the large outlay which has been made on that barren place. The sportsmen here are all in their glory, there being lots of pheasant, woodcock, snipe and wildfowl. A friend of mine of the 55th killed 15 couple of woodcock, and at their Mess on Xmas Day they had 50 on their table at once. I wish I could transfer some of them to Warwick as I recollect my mother used to be exceedingly fond of them.

I find I have now been absent from you for five years, so I may calculate safely on joining you again as soon as this business is over, and if our expectations of Prize Money are half realized I shall have no difficulty as far as money goes, but at the rate we are progressing now it will take half a century to terminate so I must rest satisfied and look forward to the time when I shall be entitled to my furlough.[1]

---

1. *Wyndham Baker did not, in fact, see his home again for a further 22 years.*

I am keeping house here with a friend of the Engineer's and have everything quite in the English fashion, fireplace, papered rooms etc., and it is the best conducted and most hospitable establishment in this place.

Our Colonel (Montgomerie) who has been away some time sick, has just rejoined us, much to our satisfaction as he is a fine sensible fellow and looked up to by everybody wherever he goes.

I think next season will give quite a different character to the Expedition as we shall no longer be dependent on the shipping when we once penetrate into the Interior, but I do not think our leaders will risk an advance on the capital, till large reinforcements arrive, as we know the Chinese are making most extraordinary exertions to oppose us and are collecting armies sufficient to eat us in a week.

Tien-tsin, the key of the River leading to Peking, is fortified they say after a new manner and deemed by them perfectly impregnable.

City of Ningpo.
January 29th, 1842.

...Affairs in China continue pretty much in the same state and there is not the slightest shadow of a chance of hostilities being discontinued. We have had some rumours from Canton of their having recommenced warlike preparations, and as the Plenip[1] has gone down to have a look at them I should not be surprised if they have again received a lesson from their breach of faith. Affairs appear so threatening in Burmah that we have almost given up all hope of any reinforcements from India; so now rely on England entirely for fresh Troops, and have only as yet heard of the 35th Foot[2] coming on from the Mauritius, which is but a weak Regiment, whereas half a dozen at least are requisite to carry on things as they should be conducted

.Before the end of the following month we expect to be on the move for Hang-chow-foo, the capital of this fine Province. The Chinese tell us an army of 30,000 men is concentrated around that City, so with our small Force we may reasonably expect a smart struggle. After that, the Yang-tse-Kiang River and the five cities on its banks will give us ample employment,

1.   *Sir Henry Pottinger.*
2.   *35th (Royal Sussex) Regiment of Foot.*

until our numbers are increased sufficiently to allow for more extended operations.

This City since our occupation has become almost deserted and it makes one quite melancholy to walk along its streets.

My health still continues excellent and hope it will bear me up through the many difficulties which I shall have to encounter in the next campaign which we are about to commence, when I may calculate being separated for weeks on end from my baggage, carrying only a portmanteau with me for bedding and everything, which is not what we call in India marching for comfort. The old General[1] sets us a capital example and must have an iron constitution to stand what he goes through. The other day in a skirmish which they had with the advanced post of the enemy, the pursuit continued through snow knee-deep, and wretchedly cold, he kept up with the Troops (on foot) and when night came on bivouacked with them without changing an article of his clothes, and only a cloak to protect himself from the cold. This is what the soldiers delight in and though he is very hasty at times towards them, his negligence of self makes up for everything else in their minds.

I went the other day to view one of the most elegantly furnished houses I have seen. The ladies' bedrooms were really most perfect, with the most beautifully carved cabinets of ebony inlaid with ivory. The house has been taken possession of by the Prize Agents and unless the owner redeems his property the whole will be sold – one of the bedsteads alone is valued at £400. The gardens are laid out with the greatest taste, with grottoes and arbours composed of rock work. They are exceedingly fond of dwarf shrubs, some of which I longed to transport to Col. B.'s garden which they would grace exceedingly.

The fishing with Cormorants, which you must often have heard of, is common in China. The other day I was an eye witness of it and it certainly was a strange proceeding. Some 8 or 10 of the birds are allowed by the keeper to jump out of the boat into the water at a time; he then watches for them to dive, secures the diver and makes him disgorge his prey, then in goes the bird again and in this manner they take hundreds a day.

Wild fowl of all kinds are in the greatest abundance here, and the sportsmen hardly deign shooting anything but pheasants and woodcocks, deeming snipe, geese, ducks and teal too common to waste powder and

---

1. *General Sir Hugh Gough. Afterwards Field-Marshal Viscount Gough, K.P., G.C.B., G.C.S.I., P.C.*

shot on, which has become of late very precious.

We all feel the want of ladies' society excessively, fancy what uncivilized brutes we must be, having been nigh two years (with the exception of a week or so at Macao), without seeing a lady, and have almost forgotten the sound of soft music, but of bugles, fifes and drums we have enough in all conscience.

I intend sending this direct by H.M.S. *Wellesley* which is just about to leave this station, much to my sorrow as I shall lose a number of friends in her, being intimately acquainted with every officer on board for a long period, and in the *Cornwallis* which relieves her I know nobody.

I wish my mother would sometimes write to me as I miss her long letters considerably.[1]

Ningpo City.
March 30th, 1842.

...The Chinese have for some time past been busily employed in concentrating a large army between this and the capital of their Province Hang-chow-foo. Their advanced posts are within a few miles distance, which has given us a good deal of annoyance as their spies are constantly frightening the good people of the town into withdrawing their supplies from the Market, so that at times we have been reduced to salt provisions. In addition to this it was always unsafe moving about as fellows in concealment were at all times ready to pounce on the unguarded and many unfortunates have been carried off in this manner, and in one or two cases our countrymen have been murdered in a most barbarous fashion.

The General during the winter made several trips into the neighbourhood hoping to catch them but only with partial success, once surprising their rearguard and killing about 100 of them. About the 8th of this month, from the deserted state of the town and poverty of the Market, it was quite evident that something was on the tapis, and we were not much surprised to learn through out spies that a grand attack was to be made on us in a few days. Our interpreters have all along been accurately informed, as traitors are

---

1. *This produced a slightly indignant reply. A number of her letters were lost, and it was said that since they were clearly written, ill-disposed persons had opened them on the way just to see what was inside.*

always to be found where money is plentiful, and summing up the various reports we were warned that on the night of the 9th we should certainly be attacked.

The General was over at Chusan, so the command developed on the next senior officer, who placed little credit on these reports and did not reinforce any of the guards. In such an extended line of works as enclose this city, it is of course out of the question with our small force to attempt to keep up a line of sentries all round its walls. We have therefore only guards at the gates whose duty it is to patrol frequently during the night, through the streets in the neighbourhood. But as the guards are so widely separated from each other, I think it was wrong in not strengthening them on the night in question. Some random shots were fired at about midnight and being on duty I got up immediately and took out a picquet to see what was the matter. After an hour's walk I returned quite satisfied that it was merely a shot fired at a junk (by one of the men-of-war) trying to make her escape, but it afterwards proved to have been a shot fired by the *Columbine*, from our bank of the river at only 100 yards distance.

I had hardly got to bed again when a regular cannonading commenced, the Alarm sounded and of course we were at our posts almost immediately. Our worthy commandant Col. Montgomerie, C.B., despatched me with a gun to defend a long street near our quarters, when in came an officer who commanded one of the most distant gates with the intelligence that he had been surrounded from the inside and outside of the City by numbers of the enemy, and seeing the utter folly of resisting such odds with the gate already forced, he deemed it prudent to retire. Seeing that no time was to be lost Col. M. moved off with a couple of guns and about 50 men to endeavour to retake the lost post, while a company was sent off to go through the streets direct to the place, a distance of about a mile. This latter party hardly proceeded 200 yards when they fell in with the victors, coming in flushed with success and eager for fresh conquests. It was still dark so our fellows remained quiet until the enemy were close to them, when they let fly with certainty, this was so unexpected that they turned immediately, closely followed by our old soldiers who continued to lessen their numbers still more in the flight. A few minutes after this Col. M. joined, and hearing continued firing at the next gate he hastened on to their relief. The Guard had been attacked at the commencement and he arrived very opportunely as their ammunition was running short. Nothing could be more gallant than the conduct of the enemy in endeavouring to force this gateway, only a few men could act at the same time on the door which was completely exposed to our

Musketry, so that it was almost certain death making the attempt. The assailants had already lost many men, still others came on undauntedly, and of course in the long run our ammunition would have failed and the guard been lost, if it had not been for the timely arrival of Col. M.'s party. The street leading directly to the gate (it now being near dawn) was thronged with soldiers, but a few rounds of shrapnel soon forced them to fall back to the corner of the street where they were protected from view. Col. M. was here slightly wounded but determined on following them up with as large a party as could be mustered, which amounted to about 100 men. On getting to the turning of the street, their numbers appeared most formidable, forming a dense mass as far as they eye could reach and as we afterwards learnt consisted of 5,000 men. The Col. apprehended they would make a rush on our little party with their spears, which had they done they must have totally annihilated the Party. The enemy seemed determined on standing, so Col. M. moved up to within 20 paces of them so that not a shot could possibly fail. The men nearest our party were cutting about with their swords and brandishing their spears in the most ridiculous manner, and were so crammed up by those in the rear eager to display their courage that had they been ever so anxious to retire it was now quite impossible. Some fine Mandarins on horseback were seen inciting them to advance which was now the only way open to them, but at this moment the gun opened and the Infantry started firing; those in front fell so thick that there was no facing such a storm, the firing lasted only about five minutes at the utmost and in that time 200 of the *celestials* had fallen in the space of 36 measured paces.

Old Peninsular men who had seen many hard fought fields say they never saw so many bodies in so confined a space. I for one never beheld anything so awfully shocking, killed and wounded lay promiscuously four deep and in one spot we found a horse untouched, but unable to rise from the pressure of dead and dying above him. The pursuit continued for seven miles; many of them, too fatigued to go on, drowned themselves rather than give themselves up, and of course many were killed besides, so that altogether at the gateway 600 must have perished, six times the strength of ourselves.

Whilst all this had been going forward an attack on the shipping by batteries on the river bank and rafts was likewise going forward. This is the first time during the war that the Chinese have acted on the offensive, and though the attack was well planned and bravely conducted, yet never was anything so ineffectual. At the same time as they were attacking us a similar affair was going on at Shanghai which ended alike unsuccessfully.

The Division which formed the attacking part on this occasion was composed of men from the very borders of Turkestan. It is now totally broken up and disorganized and will probably never be brought against us again.

> On Board the Transport *Palmyra*,
> Off the Rugged Islands.
> June 1st, 1842.

We were allowed to remain unmolested during the interval between the 4th of April and our departure from the city of Ningpo on the 6th of May. I suppose the people saw the utter uselessness of any further attempt to expel us from the city, but they continued to harass us by carrying off soldiers who ventured out unarmed, in most instances the unfortunate victims were murdered in the most barbarous manner. On one occasion a man who was missing was traced to a Chinaman's house where he was in the habit of going for liquor. After rummaging every hole and corner they came across a suspicious looking sack, which on examination contained the poor fellow's headless body cut and gashed all over. In the confusion of the search the man of the house had escaped, but the exasperated comrades of the deceased took their vengeance on the spot by firing the house. On another occasion the same kind of thing occurred and we retaliated by burning all the buildings in the neighbourhood, so I hope it will show them what a losing concern such a cowardly system is. In addition to the annoyance caused by losing men in this way, it renders the men most inhuman when they fall in with the enemy; so much so, that the other day the greatest difficulty was experienced in preventing the soldiers from firing on the Chinese after they had laid down their arms and were supplicating for mercy. The British common soldier in fact is a strange compound, for they are very kind to their prisoners when once the excitement ceases.

On the 6th of May the arrangements for our embarkation were all completed and not the slightest disturbance occurred. The General, apprehensive that on our departure the rabble of the town would destroy all the buildings we had guarded during our stay, summoned all the respectable Chinamen he could get together and desired them to take over charge from us. They got together a few militia and actually relieved our Guards and thanked the General saying the treatment they had received from us during our occupation of the city was in all respects better than they had a right to expect.

The steamers took us down to our Transports waiting at Chusan and you may be sure we were all heartily delighted at once more making a move after being idle so long at that place Ningpo.

After a delay of six days we at length got under weigh and proceeded to the north, and although the distance to Chapoo is only some 56 or 60 miles, we did not reach that place till the 17th of May. Chapoo you must know is on the left bank of the Hang-chow-foo river, just at its entrance, and supposed to be a place of considerable importance from the great trade which it carried on with the opposite continent of Japan. The junks seemed to have had timely warning of our approach as few were found there on our arrival and those full of munitions of war which we accordingly burnt when they fell into our possession. We fixed on a beautiful little bay to land in, which we effected with capital order and expedition early in the morning.

No opposition was offered to us on disembarking, indeed we were quite out of their range and considerably to the right of their fortified positions on the heights. This was intentional, to enable us to completely outflank as we had done on all occasions so successfully before, whilst the Men-of-War were occupying their attention in front by pounding away at the Batteries. After exchanging a few volleys with the head of each column as they came into view they fell back on their city for protection, some two or three hundred who had imprudently delayed longer than their less courageous comrades at length fled, but found to their dismay their retreat intercepted by our flank movement, they therefore threw themselves into a large isolated building which they defended in the most determined manner for more than an hour. The house was at last set on fire and most of those who still survived preferred perishing in its ruins to falling into our hands. At this place I lost two friends, Col. Tomlinson of the 18th,[1] a most gallant, excellent fellow and Col. A. Trings who fell at the head of his party when endeavouring to force an entrance into the building. Capt. Campbell of the 55th[2] was also killed. Altogether at this insignificant little place our loss was very great, as besides those mentioned 45 to 50 men and officers were rendered *hors-de-combat.*

We entered the city without any further opposition and the Artillery did here what I believe they have seldom done before and what was greatly

1.   *18th (The Royal Irish) Regiment of Foot.*
2.   *55th (The Westmorland) Regiment of Foot.*

applauded by the lookers on. We actually, by main force, dragged our guns up the steep face of the ramparts at the same time as the Infantry were scaling them with some difficulty. The town itself is smaller than Ningpo, being barely three miles round the walls. Inside the town a walled enclosure was found occupied exclusively by the Tartar garrison.

William C. Hunter records that an English officer who was present at the taking of Chapoo in May 1842, said: "After the city had been captured, I entered more than 100 houses, and in each there were not less than two, and in many were as many as eight persons found dead. They were the bodies of mothers and daughters who had committed suicide from a dread of becoming prisoners; 1600 were buried after the battle, of which more than half were Tartar soldiers, who in despair of killing the enemy, and prefering death to defeat, had nearly all destroyed themselves."

While Basil Lubbock tells us that: "not only canals, but the drinking wells were found to be crammed with the bodies of women and children. Yet Sir Hugh Gough would allow no looting, and the greatest attention was shown to Chinese prisoners and wounded, and when our forces left the town, prisoners were released, and each of the wounded Chinese presented with money, (about three dollars per man). Yet Elepoo, the high-minded Lt.-General of Chapoo, was punished and disgraced by the Emperor, for giving up Anstruther of the Madras Artillery (Wyndham's Regiment), Mrs Noble and Lt. Douglas."

Wyndham Baker continues:

> I never saw any Tartar females before; they differ considerably from the Chinese, being much fairer and with finer features and all of them allow their feet to grow to normal size.
>
> There appeared to be very little friendship between the Chinese and their former conquerors, as one may judge from the little consideration shown towards the dying and wounded, lying about close to their houses, beseeching for water, which they were more likely to get from our hands than the Chinese. The Chinese must have been plundering the Tartar city as soon as the fight commenced, as when we entered, it was most thoroughly sacked, and the Chinese were going away loaded in every direction.
>
> The country round Chapoo beats anything we have yet seen, indeed I

defy anything to equal it in beauty – one immense valley as far as the eye could reach, covered with the most luxurious vegetation, with the people going on with their work in the fields quite unconcerned. I noticed the vine, mulberry, peach, plum, and numerous other fruits growing almost wild everywhere, and at this time, being in full blossom, they added much to the beauty of the scene.

From Chapoo, it was at first intended we should have gone and attacked Hang-chow-foo, but the approach by the river was pronounced quite impracticable by the surveyors, and with barely 2,500 men it was considered imprudent advancing against a city very little inferior to London in size and population, 70 miles from our ships, and without any possible way of transporting heavy Artillery, which of course we could hardly have dared going without. The mosquitoes were most annoying at Chapoo, which made me determined to carry nets at all costs.

Before quitting Chapoo, the Admiral[1] despatched a light surveying squadron to inspect the entrance to the Yang-tse-Kiang and to return and report to him here. It behoved us to be cautious hereabouts as very little is known of this part of the coast, and we were obliged to come to anchor every night, for fear, if we stood, of coming in contact of some island in the dark, before unknown.

Under the Walls of Nanking.
August 30th, 1842.

My dear Mother & Sisters,

Although only allowed a few minutes, I am determined on writing to you, if it be only to acquaint you with my wellbeing, of which, for the long interval which has taken place since I last wrote, you may begin to feel some doubts. Had I the time I should not be able to give you long accounts of the events which have lately come under my observation, as almost every instant is occupied in some way or another, but when I return to the ship I hope to have more time to write to you at more length.

I enclose a chip of the Porcelain Tower,[2] which far surpasses everything we have heard about it. It is 10 miles hence and I was the fourth to visit it.

The Treaty[3] was signed and sealed yesterday on board H.M.S. *Cornwallis.*

1. *Admiral Sir William Parker, G.C.B.*
2. *The Treaty of Nanking.*
3. *From Basil Lubbock's book "The Opium Clippers".*

"At the end of the war[1] the *Nemesis* hurried off to Formosa in the hopes of being able to save the survivors of the ill-fated *Ann* and *Nerbudda* who had been ship-wrecked, but only a few were found still alive, – and it was thought reserved for special torture."

"The most conspicuous building at Nanking was the famous Porcelain Tower built by the Emperor Yung-lo, 1403–1428 (in memory of his Mother, in a moment of filial piety!). The Pagoda was an octagon and was about 260 feet high. The outer walls were encased in bricks of the finest porcelain, and each of the nine storeys in which the building was divided, was marked by eaves composed of glazed tiles of the same material. Hung on chains which stretched from the six apexes of the eaves of the roof, were five pearls of 'good augury' for the city's safety, – from flood, fire, storm and civil disturbance.

"Nanking was formerly one of the chief literary centres of the Empire. It was taken by the British in 1842 and made a Treaty port in 1848, but was not formerly opened. Its proximity to Che-Kiang, where the trade was stopped while Nanking was still in the hands of the rebels, made it's opening a difficult matter. In 1895 it was voluntarily thrown open to foreign trade by the Chinese government, and in 1909 it was connected by railway with Shanghai. Satin, crepe, nankeen cloth, paper, pottery and artificial flowers were among its chief manufactures. There is a depth of some 17–45 feet at the quays, and all vessels can reach Nanking if they are able to pass the flats at the mouth of the Yang-tse. The town imports cotton goods and yarn, metals etc."

1.. *The Porcelain Tower and the story of Nanking from the "Encyclopedia Britannica".*

On Board The *Lady Flora*, off Nanking.
September 17th, 1842.

To his dear mother & sisters,

My last letter was written to you before we entered this river from a place called the Rugged Islands. Before that I had a piece of good fortune. When our Reinforcements arrived in June, the force had become too unwieldly to manage altogether, so it was broken up into Brigades and the Artillery Arm became a distinct command, and Col. Montgomerie most handsomely conferred the Adjutancy of the Corps to me. Since that I have been almost incessantly employed in superintending, rationing, correspondence, drilling and a thousand other things connected with 1,200 men.

(I meant to tell you in my last letter that you will see honourable mention made of me in the Despatches, which I am conceited enough to consider on the occasion in question only my desert. I escaped twice, most narrowly with my life, but only received contusions, which are not reckoned).

My present salary is handsome, being upwards of £20 per annum, exclusive of my regular pay. I should be better pleased if I could command a little more leisure – if it were only to write a little oftener to you.

After advancing very cautiously, we at length made the entrance of this notable river on the 13th of June. The appearance of the country on either side was anything but prepossessing as we went along, being very flat and uninteresting, with only a few fishermen's huts. The river gradually narrowed all the way up to Woosung, at which place the Fleet anchored off the day of our entering the river, thus accomplishing what we calculated would take a fortnight in one day. The river was about four miles wide!

Woosung is a place of very minor consideration, but its situation, like that of Chinghai which we attacked last year, is everything. It stands on the right or southern bank of the river at the immediate entrance of a smaller river from which it takes its name. It is the key to a city of great magnitude and commercial importance called Shanghai. The Chinese seemed to be fully sensible of the value of the position and had lavished considerable money and labour in throwing up all kinds of defences at the entrance to this river and Batteries were even more extensive than at Amoy or Chusan. A delay occurred of one or two days to enable the surveyors to select a good berth for the Men-of-War to bombard the whole line.

The Chinese appear to have attributed the delay to fear, as they sent off a message that they were prepared and wished to know what hindered us, and even when the boats were laying down buoys to guide the Men-of-War into their positions, the enemy set up cheers of defiance, so confident did they appear in their own strength. They were not allowed to indulge long in these ideas as the ships were towed into their places on the morning of the 16th, under a pretty well sustained fire from the Batteries, which was suffered to pass unnoticed until the vessels came to anchor. It took them about three hours to clear the Batteries and the firing was pretty heavy on both sides, but being out of range of their fire I hardly felt the interest that I did on the occasion of Ching-hai and Amoy when there was some excitement to hear the shot whizzing over you. Woosung was in some measure a failure, as when the Navy had practically cleared the Batteries it was high time for the military to come into play, but instead of which the Admiral and all his Marines landed, and it was only on their receiving a slight check, that the steamers were dispatched for us. In the mean time the enemy withdrew and we landed too late for anything. The Navy suffered a little damage, but the Chinese never escaped so well off before. A vast number of brass and iron guns were here captured, quite recently cast, and on these were inscribed the most ridiculous mottoes such as "Tamer of Barbarians", "Scourge of Foreigners", etc. On the 19th we pushed on towards Shanghai, where we expected a smart resistance, having received reports of fugitives from Woosung having rallied and joined the garrison there.

The land party under the command of Col. Montgomerie, with all the Artillery, a portion of H.M.'s 18th and 49th Rifles and Sappers,[1] set out accordingly early in the morning, whilst the remainder of the Troops were to go up by water, after the most harassing day's work I ever recollect.

The weather was exceedingly warm and the roads bad, so that the guns were upset times out of number and the horses taken out of the harness, to drag the guns by hand over very bad places, I should say 60 times at least, until we at length drew near the city. Horses and men were completely overpowered by fatigue, and we were debating whether it was possible to move further when a cannonading was heard in the direction of the river, as if by magic everyone jumped up.

At this time we were moving parallel to the shipping[2] in the river at about a mile distance away. Unfortunately, a line of Battery extended some way along the bank between us and the shipping. We were not seen from the

---

1. *49th (the Hertfordshire) Regiment of Foot (became the Royal Berkshire Regiment).*
2. *H.M. Fleet and Transports.*

shipping who endeavoured to dismantle these works as they passed up and their shells fell amongst us most disgracefully, but not a man was touched. We at length came to the walls which we found in possession of our skirmishers who were in advance of us. The gates were strongly guarded and the rest of the Troops betook themselves to the nearest houses as quarters for the night. We very fortunately got into a Pawnbroker's shop on a scale of great magnificence, where one is used to nothing but filth and poverty in connection with the trade in England, in China sometimes the highest Mandarins are proprietors of these lucrative concerns. The house we entered had been plundered by the mob before we arrived but even then there were plenty of handsome silks and satins and silver trinkets. About seven o'clock that night we sat down to breakfast, being the first time that day we had eaten. On the road I had sustained myself with a cigar. I happened to be on duty and was therefore required to be on the alert during the night and as a fire broke out close to our quarters, little sleep was permitted me that night.

Shanghai with its wide streets appeared a fine city. The trade carried on here must be very considerable as the river was crowded with junks trading to and from all parts of China and some were taking cargoes for our possession in the Straits. The steamers penetrated several miles up a river and at one time they believed they were close to the celebrated city of Soo-chow-foo, when the shallowness of the water prevented their further progress. We were all much interested in the success of this trip as we should have attacked Soo-chow-foo could we have reached it, as it is said by all Chinese to be the Paradise of China we all looked forward to seeing its wonders.

Our sojourn here was very brief as we returned by the same road, sending the guns down in the steamers so that we had a more agreeable march going back.

At Woosung a number of very curiously constructed boats were discovered, fitted with paddle wheels turned by a winch and evidently intended as imitations of our steamers; with four men working at the winch, the boat was propelled along at the rate of three or four miles an hour. I hope one of these may be sent home to England with its little guns and all complete.

From Mr. Raymond Dawson's book "The Legacy of China", there is an interesting account of Chinese paddle-wheel boats. He says: "Descriptions of treadmill-operated paddle-wheel boats begin to appear in Chinese literature in the 5th and 6th Centuries A.D., until by 1130 government battleships with as many as 23 wheels were constructed by a Naval architect named Kao Hsüan. Paddle-wheel warships continued to be of much importance for guarding the Yangtse against Chinese Tartars... During the Opium Wars 1839-42 a considerable number of treadmill-operated paddle-wheel war junks were sent against the British ships and gave a good account of themselves, although their cause was hopeless."

Wyndham continues:

> It was just at this time that the Plenip. Lord Saltoun and the reinforcements from India and England joined us. Lord Saltoun is a mild, good-natured kind of old gentleman, with an extraordinary predilection for music, for which he professes great talent and plays two or three instruments exceedingly well.[1] He appears very much disgusted at having come out here.
>
> At Woosung a Man-of-War was considered sufficient to blockade the river we had just left, so on the 6th of July we all made another start and the Fleet now amounted to upwards of 70 sail and when all under canvas it was a sight well worth beholding. As we advanced the country was much prettier, with here and there a stately Pagoda to mark the burial place of some long-forgotten Mandarin. We never continued under sail after dark but always anchored in the afternoon. The people busy in their fields, who could never in their lives have seen a European vessel, treated us with the greatest apathy. After some slight delays occurring where the passage was unusually intricate, we at length caught sight of *Golden Island* on the 20th of July. It is only about 100 miles from *Woosung* and we had been a fortnight about it, which for river work is tolerably good going. The Admiral and General were a day or two in advance of us, and from what information they had been able to glean from interpreters, there appeared little likelihood of our encountering any opposition either at Golden Island or the neighbouring town of Ching-kiang-foo. The great Imperial Canal flows under its walls from which I suppose it derives its great opulence and importance. The evening

---

1. *A refreshingly youthful tribute to Lt. Gen. Alexander George, 16th Lord Saltoun, K.T.K.C.B., G.C.H., who had fought in the Peninsula War 1811–1814, at Quatre Bras and at Waterloo. By Permission of G. Blackwood.*

of our arrival here I formed a party to visit the Island. We found it completely inhabited with Chinese priests who showed us the wonders of the place most willingly. The Temples were numerous and large and I obtained an excellent view of the city by means of my telescope from the top of the Pagoda.

On my return to the ship I found orders had been issued for the whole of the Troops to be held in readiness to land by daylight, so it behoved us, the Artillery, to set to work to get the guns ready. I was occupied till long after midnight and had to be ready for disembarkation by four in the morning. The 21st of July happened to be the anniversary of my escape last year in the typhoon, so I did not regard it as a propitious day.

The boats of the *Blonde* came to land the guns; our party consisted of about 45 artillery men, 2 heavy howitzers with about 100 helpless natives to assist in carrying the shot boxes. Major Blundell commanding the party and myself and his staff were in the front boat, a stout-build pinnace with a crew of 12 hands besides the officer, and Lt. Crouch who had charge of all the boats on the occasion. We soon joined the entrance to the Canal and proceeded leisurely to enable the heavily laden boats to keep up with us. In all we mustered four Men-of-War boats and two Transports, one of the latter, a heavy boat, contained our guns and ammunition besides a portion of the men.

We were about 100 yards in front of the other boats when in turning an angle in the Canal we suddenly came in view of the walls from which we were hardly musketry range distant; I could not help remarking that they appeared much more formidable showing evident signs of recent repair. A large gateway was directly in front with the Canal beneath it and a handsome bridge across connecting the suburbs and the town. I had just selected a good spot for disembarking the guns, when I beheld on the walls a number of Chinese soldiers handling their matchlocks in a manner not likely to be mistaken and we were instantly saluted with a volley. We hailed the boats to turn about and were too close to use the gun in the bow of our boat being unable to give it sufficient elevation to reach the top of the walls. The seamen were provided with muskets which they used, but ineffectually as the defenders were wholly sheltered by the parapet whilst we were completely exposed. The men fell fast, which of course emboldened the enemy, poor Crouch fell wounded across me and I thought would have died, but we staunched the wound and he recovered sufficiently to give directions. A light boat of the *Blonde* got between us and the arch where she was comparatively safe, and to her we transferred the wounded, and seeing that if we remained longer where we were, every one of the party would be sacrificed, I persuaded Crouch to try and get the boat into the bank and allow the few who remained to land; this we did while the Chinese like infuriated demons set up a shout. On mustering the remnant of the party the Major and myself and two seamen were the only persons who remained unwounded, Crouch received two more wounds and it was with the utmost difficulty that we dragged him along. On reaching the other boats further down the stream we found they were under the opposite bank, but the transport with the guns had been cut adrift the moment the firing commenced and now a friendly current brought her towards us. Attempts to land the guns were made but it was quite impossible as the enemy had our range so completely. Thinking it highly probable the enemy would sally out on us, it was considered most prudent to withdraw with the wounded.

The Major and I at once proceeded on board the *Cornwallis* (the Flagship) to solicit some assistance to enable us to recover our losses. 200 Marines and about the same number of Sepoys were immediately placed at our disposal and being provided with scaling ladders we determined to hazard an attack on the portion of the town where we had been before so warmly received. I think by nature I am very cool, but for this attack I wrought up to the highest pitch of excitement. The disposition of our little force having been arranged by Major Blundell, I proceeded in advance as guide. We continued parallel to the Canal for some distance, then diverged to the left which brought us close to the wall about 200 yards from the bridge. A brisk fire was kept up on the head of our column but the men were speedily put into houses close by where they were but little exposed and could fire at their ease, in this manner we got from house to house close underneath the wall. In reconnoitring I perceived that some of our people were already in possession of the Walls and were hurrying in our direction. Our marksmen from the houses having to all appearances done their duty and nigh cleared the Walls of its defenders, we pushed forward with ladders to storm, but the Walls were very high and the ladders did not reach within 4½ feet of the top. Seeing that delay for a moment longer was dangerous, I jumped up the ladder and gained the Wall in safety. Watson of the Navy, a most intimate friend of mine, following close on my heels. I was just down inside when I perceived that the enemy were close behind on either Wall and were deliberately aiming at us. My foot just touched the ground when I received a blow which sent me senseless to the ground. Watson followed my example. (Three balls passed through his jacket.) I forget what passed for the next two minutes but I recollect a Marine tumbling dead over me, then Captain

Richards got me away and in a short time I recovered. To conclude the day's work at Ching-kiang-foo, I must tell you that we soon mustered pretty strong inside and were preparing to make a push at their stronghold when an awful explosion took place and in rushed Brig. Bartley's Brigade and the few defenders remaining were speedily overpowered.

This gateway was exceedingly strong with three inner enclosures. Bartley, not aware of our being inside so near him, had permitted the engineers to creep over our bridge and fix the powder bags on the gate, which was shattered to atoms by the explosion, thus enabling a large column of Infantry to pour in simultaneously without any obstruction.

Meanwhile Lord Saltoun and his Brigade attacked the Chinese in their entrenchments outside the Walls without any loss hardly. The Men-of-War were too far off to participate in the day's work, but one or two steamers got as close in as possible and did good work by letting off a few shells which distracted the attention of the enemy from the storming party, just before the assault.

It is calculated that the Chinese met us here on very nearly equal terms as regards numbers; we had 7,500 men landed and the Chinese statements will not account for quite so many on either side. Our loss was more severe than on any previous occasion, amounting in killed and wounded to nearly 200 men.

At Ching-kiang-foo we got little as the Chinese had plundered everything themselves before we entered, but by the rules of warfare the soldier had a fair right here to pillage, it being a case of "Capture by Assault", which in the Peninsula was considered a just claim.

We were delayed until the 4th of August when we again made a start, expecting to reach Nanking, a distance of 45 miles, in a day or two, but such was the force of the current, that sometimes with a fair wind and all the sail we could carry, we could hardly make way against it. On the 7th we sighted the far-famed Porcelain Tower of Nanking and on the 8th anchored within two miles of the Walls of Nanking, which were plainly visible from our docks, thickly crowded with soldiers and tents.

On the 9th I accompanied Col. Montgomerie and a party of engineers for the purpose of reconnoitring. We started very early so as to land by daylight and proceeded down a fine creek which brought us abreast of some high hills. These commanded a good view of the walls whose extent seemed unbounded, besides which they were very high and thick. We also found a most admirable road leading to one of the Gates of the City. In returning to our boats the remains of an old Wall were pointed out as being the outer

Wall of the old city of Nanking, which nearly encircles the present city all round. I have come across traces of it but not a remnant remains of the town. In our excursion we passed through orchards of pomegranates and Spanish chestnuts growing wild.

When the General received Col. M.'s report he at once determined on making his principal attack from the side we had reconnoitred and we accordingly commenced disembarking our siege train. The General stated it as his determination in this instance to give the Artillery fair play, and gave us a certain time to effect a breach before he brought forward the Infantry. We were all delighted with this project and set to work with a good will to get the ordnance into position, and had soon got up all our guns ready for the attack when an order arrived from the Plenip. to cease hostilities.

It appears that immediately on our arrival here, Mandarins visited the Plenip. and were exceedingly desirous to treat, but not being satisified with their powers, he gave them to understand that until they produced more complete qualifications, he would have nothing to say to them, and would not till then interfere with the offensive operations in progress. This decided conduct on the Plenip.'s part changed their conduct immediately and in a few days they produced the most ample powers from the Emperor. Meetings took place daily between the Plenip. and the High Imperial Commissioners. It was quite evident that the Chinese were no longer insincere in their wishes for peace. The claims of the British Government were distinctly stated and every point readily acceded to, but we felt some doubts about the Emperor ratifying the terms which his delegates had accepted. In this, however, we were mistaken as The Treaty has been duly signed and sealed by the proud old Tartar who must have been very loath after all his threats to succumb to our demands.

For THE TREATY OF NANKING the terms are, as nearly as I can understand, briefly as follows:-

(1)   The cession of the Island of Hong Kong to the British Crown.

(2)   An indemnity to the British Government of six million of dollars, to be paid before we evacuate the river. (Most of this is already paid.)

(3)   A further sum of 15 millions to be paid within three years, during which time Chusan and Amoy will be returned, and unless the above be paid within the time specified, those places will be ever afterwards held by the British.

(4)   Official intercourse to be carried on between the two countries on equal footing.

(5)   Consuls to reside in Shanghai, Ningpo, Foochow-foo, Amoy and
       Canton, which are to be considered open ports.

There are some other points which are of minor importance. The opium
question seemed to embarrass them more than any other and they could
not understand why we could not put a stop to it if we felt so inclined. The
Plenip. explained to them that even if we prevented our merchants from
trading in the drug it would have no effect on other nations, but that as long
as the demand continued so long would opium be ready for sale and said
that in our own country we could not keep out spirits but the government
allowed them to be imported, though so highly taxed as to be a great source
of Revenue to the Crown, and he recommended the Chinese doing the
same with regard to opium. They comprehended this, but thought the
remedy would hardly answer, as they knew the higher the article was taxed,
the greater would be the inducement to smugglers to get it into the country
free of duty. It has evidently occupied much of their consideration and until
they can establish an efficient coastguard they will continue to suffer from
this evil.

The war has at last come to a termination and contrary to all opinions we
have finished by getting the most advantageous terms, and I trust on the
receipt of the money in England, the heart of John Bull will be liberal towards
the Army and Navy, whose deserts have hitherto been but poorly requited.

Hoping you are all well at home and with my best love to everyone.

Believe me,
            Yours most affectionately,
                Wyndham Baker.

P.S. I had the pleasure of attending a ceremonial conference between the
Plenip. and the Commissioners. After landing we passed through a line of
soldiers without arms, and beyond came to some courtyards with more
soldiers, who received us with bands playing and colours flying, their music
was most barbarous. At length we came to a large building where
Mandarins were waiting to welcome us to the banquet. Joints and
sweetmeats were all they feasted us with, but they were served up in a tasty
and elegant fashion. The Chinese had never before seen us in our uniform
and as many of the dresses were on this occasion exceedingly handsome,
they excited much admiration. The Mandarins were lost in astonishment at

our fine Arab horses and said they had never before seen such beautiful animals.

Nothing keeps us here now, so I suppose we shall make the best of our way down the river in a few days and when we arrive at Chusan there will be a regular dispersion of the force, some to remain there, others to relieve those now at Amoy, some to garrison Hong-Kong, and the remainder to India with all speed.

Now that I am about to leave China I shall do so with regret as there are many points about the Chinese which I like exceedingly and would prefer this country infinitely to India if we had a little more society. The Chinese themselves are a very powerful race and are very fine fellows compared with the effeminate natives of India and would make such perfect soldiers if properly taken in hand.

Undated letter from China, about October 1842, Ningpo.

I think I may commence my narrative from the date of my last letter to you in September, just before our leaving the neighbourhood of that celebrated place Nanking.

The Treaty having been duly signed (contrary to the opinion of all the knowing ones) by the Representatives of the two nations, we prepared to leave the River Yangtse-Kiang, but our passage down the River, though an extremely difficult and hazardous undertaking, was attempted with much good luck.

When we took our departure from Nanking, the rainy season seemed to just have commenced. The river was consequently much swollen and in many places had overflown its banks to such an extent as to render it almost impossible to recognize the directing points by which we had steered on our way up the river a month or so previously. The current which we had easily stemmed then with a light wind, had now become a raging torrent, such as wholly to defy anything but steam to make head against it. Being in our favour, however, we calculated much on its friendly assistance, but soon found that we would gladly have been without it, as its impetuosity rendered the ship almost wholly unmanageable and was sweeping us into some new danger or other.

The crew of the Transport in which I happened to be were all Europeans, but so sickly just at this time when their help was so necessary, as to be unable to show a man up on deck with the exception of the Captain himself

– officers and all were sick – yet notwithstanding all these difficulties, by extraordinary good fortune we got safely down the river.

Our manner of proceeding was to me of the most novel description but I fear I shall hardly be able to explain it to unnautical people like yourselves, but I will endeavour to do so. Having no men to go aloft to loosen or take in the sails, it was out of the question sailing; if we got up the anchor which our soldiers could easily do, we immediately became at the mercy of the current, we therefore kept the anchor so that as almost always to touch the ground and by shifting the helm to and fro we were able to drop the ship about a mile or so an hour – in this manner we travelled backwards all the way down. A boat was kept towing about 100 fathoms further astern of us with a man to sound and give warning of any approaching danger, when we immediately called a halt by putting the helm amidships.

Ford, who was the Captain of his ship, and a fine seaman of great experience, said he never could have believed he could have brought down his ship in such a manner

I regretted the termination of the War, as I looked at one time most sanguinely forward to visiting Peking, but I think now it is just as well as it is, and I feel much pleasure in having seen the War at length terminated by a very satisfactory treaty under the walls of their ancient capital.

To proceed with my narrative I must tell you that after many dangers and difficulties, which considering our sickly state we got through wonderfully well, we at last got down to Woosung, but being afraid to venture to sea in our then helpless condition, we delayed there some days, hoping some of the Men-of-War would take pity on us and grant us the assistance of a few hands to navigate the ship. Unfortunately, they were all as bad if not worse off than ourselves, so we were at length compelled to put to sea relying on our own resources entirely. Since our arrival at Woosung on first entering the river in June, we had used no other water but what we got alongside for the trouble of drawing, and the soldiers and sailors would always insist upon in that the water of the river which they drank was the cause of all their sickness. Whether this was the cause or not I will not attempt to say, but I know full well in cholera and all epidemics that I have seen anything of, a great deal depends on the imagination of the sufferers. At this time the men had completely lost heart and were dying very fast, their constitutions being completely worn out by constant attacks of fever and ague and dysentry, and the men looked like living skeletons and were hardly able to crawl about the deck. I frequently used to be amongst them and endeavoured to do all I could to keep up their spirits, but they used to say they would never be better till they got clear of the river. On the 13th of October we at last got into salt water again and it was immediately observed that the men began to recover as if by magic, and one hospital was soon clean of all the bad cases.

I have been in as many uncomfortable situations as most fellows, but I think for 10 days together I have never been in such an uncomfortable plight as I was in that river, and am quite convinced that if my mind had not been constantly occupied with other matters I should have been seriously ill. As it was I escaped the fever almost entirely and with the exception of the Captain suffered less than anyone on board. By excessive good luck we had a favourable breeze all the way to Chusan, where we arrived without any further accident on the 18th of October.

Our stay was delayed from day to day in consequence of alterations being made in the force to be left here in garrison and as every change in the Artillery obliged me to commence work afresh I was pretty fully engulfed. When I could snatch an hour for recreation I started on shore for a walk and as the winter was now setting in I enjoyed a good walk amazingly on this really beautiful island; if we ever give it up to the Chinese I shall be very sorry as it was to my mind the jolliest and most hospitable place I had seen in China. The people here have grown to become so well acquainted with our habits and are apparently so fond of us, that I think the Mandarins will never again be able to stop our supplies or set the people against us as they did formerly. T'was the middle of November before all our arrangements were completed and we were able to quit for the southward, and a few days agreeable sailing without any adventure brought us to Hongkong, from which place I had been absent about 15 months. In that time it had become a town of importance, whereas when I left it there were only a few fishermen's houses made of mud.

I think the English merchants in China,[1] with Jardine's House at their head, are the most enterprising people that I have ever come across and there is nothing they would be afraid to undertake. Here, for instance, before Hong-kong had been ceded to us, we found the merchants all established and building on every spot. Gold here seemed to be made with the same ease, and thought of in the same ratio as silver is in England, and their hospitality is unbounded.

1.   *"The success of the coastal trade in the 1830s was attributable among other factors, to the uncommon qualities of William Jardine, and the zeal of his Captains. Judging by the voluminous letters sent to the Captains from Canton, Jardine no doubt won their trust and devotion by always taking care of their personal interests with the utmost care and generosity. With unusual vision and remarkable efficiency, he speculated in the Opium*

When at Macao in July 1837, I stayed with a family of the name of Leighton, whom I think I mentioned in one of my letters as having made a fortune in some opium speculation in an incredible short space of time. On my enquiry for them on my return on this occasion, I found him a Bankrupt without a sixpence to his name and his house and furniture, of the most costly and elegant description, just going to the hammer.

I thought at one moment that War would have recommenced, as in consequence of a riot at Canton we were on the point of moving up the whole Force, which had we done I think there is little doubt we should have come to blows and perhaps the Treaty would have been upset and we should have had the whole thing to do over again. It is very evident that we are still extremely unpopular down near Canton and the Government have had quite enough of our company at present, though I dare say in a few years they will get over their fright and meet us on more equal terms. You will read in the papers an account of the savage and most inhuman burden of some 200 of our prisoners (mostly shipwrecked sailors) on the Island of Formosa.

I traced a box sent to me with a number of useful things in it, as far as Singapore, but fear it must have found its way to the bottom of the sea in one of the many unfortunate shipwrecks which have lately taken place in the China Seas.

Market in Canton, supplied the ships with ample cargo, and directed the voyages of the Fleet." From "Commissioner Lin & The Opium War" by Hsin-pao Chang.

"In the private room of Doctor William Jardine there was no chair to be seen, for that energetic man objected to his time being wasted in business hours, by idlers and those who dropped in merely to have a quiet gossip.

Small wonder that he amassed a fortune running into six figures in twenty years." From "The Opium Clippers" by Basil Lubbock.

He retired from business and returned to Britain in November 1838, and was succeeded by James Matheson as head of the firm.
Basil Lubbock also says:

"The early success of Jardine, Matheson & Co. was in great part due to the charm of manner of young Matheson, as well as to his level-headed Scotch shrewdness. Born at Sherness on November 17, 1796, he was only 19 years of age when he arrived in Calcutta, and scarcely 20 when he left his Uncle's Counting House and plunged into the unknown, as China was in those days to anyone outside the Company's employ.

"Matheson was one of those wise men who studied the people amongst whom he came to live. He did all he could to help the poorer Chinese; he was one of the chief supporters of Morrison's Educational Society, for teaching young Chinese English, and it was owing to his friendship that the strange Missionery Gutzlaff, with his tracts and pills, found himself aboard the Sylph and other Opium Clippers.

"In 1827 Matheson imported the first printing press into China, and it was due to him that the Canton Register, the first English paper in China came to be printed."

"When he retired in 1842 his place in the great firm was taken by his two nephews, Alexander and Donald Matheson."
From "The Opium Clippers" by Basil Lubbock.

As I was determined not to disappoint you in the chest of tea I promised, I have selected two, one of Hysan and the other of Souchang which I have put on board.

Some of the wounded Mandarins who were taken to our hospitals for medical treatment expressed the greatest reluctance to have their wounds examined and begged to be put out of their misery as they could not bear to live after such a disgraceful defeat. Since then, they have become more reconciled to life and the kind treatment they have received from the doctors seems to astonish them exceedingly. I hope this may have a good effect in future and prevent their committing self destruction in preference to giving themselves up as prisoners.

The following day we marched to a very strong place, a kind of pass in the hills where another Division of the enemy were said to be in force, but they had prudently evacuated, leaving large stores of grain and provisions for the enemy soldiers which we destroyed, and the following day returned to Ningpo. The soldiers all made their fortunes whilst they were away as abundance of silver was found in the tents besides watches and other valuables, and the most elegant silks and satins were seen enveloping the bodies of our wretched filthy-looking followers.

> With best love to all
>> Yours most affectionately
>>> Wyndham Baker.

P.S. At the last place where we were, a proclamation was found offering a reward of 20,000 dollars for Anstruther's head, because of his "ingratitude in returning to fight them after the kind treatment he had received at Ningpo during his imprisonment."

A Summing up of the First and Second Opium Wars and the History of Chusan

From the *Encyclopedia Britannica*:

Chusan is an Island off the Chinese coast. The outermost ends of the archipelago lie across the entrance to Hangchow Bay, whose shores are becoming choked with silt from the Yangtse estuary, which opens out just to the north of them.

By reason of its character as a rocky Island and its proximity to the Yangtse estuary, Chusan Island, the chief of the Archipelago, was chosen during the Ming Dynasty, (1368–1644,) as an entrepôt for trade with Japan. Until the modern development of Japan, Japanese relations with China were naturally most intimate in the neighbourhood of the Yangtse estuary. The Japanese use of Chusan at that time is somewhat comparable to the British use of Hongkong at a later period.

In 1839–44, the West desired admission to China to market the products of their Factories and to obtain raw materials. Trouble first came from Great Britain, the European nation in which the Industrial Revolution began. On demand from British merchants, the monopoly of the Chinese trade by the English East India Company, was abolished, (1834) and friction between the English and Chinese followed.

Lord Napier was appointed the first Superintendent of British trade in Canton (1834), but Chinese officials looked upon him as a head merchant and refused to deal with him as an equal. The matter came to a head over the important question of Opium which had long been prohibited by the Chinese Government. At last Peking dispatched a special Commissioner Lin Tse-hsu, to stamp out the trade. Lin arrived at Canton in 1839. Foreign merchants were compelled to surrender their stocks of opium for destruction and pressure was put upon us not to import any more. The British objected to what seemed to them high-handed measures, and in 1839 War broke out. On August 29th, 1842, the Treaty of Nanking was signed. The Americans and French both obtained trade concessions, also later the Belgians and Swedes.

The years between 1842 and 1856, were a troubled truce. The traffic in opium continued. The Chinese violated the British flag and arrested the crew, all Chinese, on a Chinese-owned but British registered craft, the *Arrow*, on October 8, 1856. The French joined the British who were just emerging from the struggle in the Crimea and difficulties with Persia, 1856–57, and the Sepoy Mutiny which blazed out in India in 1857.

In 1857 the British and French took Canton and in the next year their Squadron ran north to Tientsin, thence to threaten Peking into submission.

On June 26th, 1857, the Treaty of Tientsin nominally closed the 2nd Opium War, but fighting continued till 1860.

The TREATY OF TIENTSIN contained the following provisions

(1) A tariff was declared and by the fixing of a rate for opium, the importation of that drug was legalized.

(2) The residence in Peking of diplomatic powers was promised.

(3) Foreigners were to be permitted to travel into the Interior.

(4) The activities of church and mission were sanctioned, and Christians, both foreign and Chinese, were guaranteed freedom in the expression of their faith.

(5) Foreign merchant vessels were allowed on the Yangtse.

(6) Several additional ports were opened to trade and foreign residents, these included Chefoo and Newchang in the north, one on Haim, two on Formosa and four on the Yangtse.

(7) Extra territory was further elaborated.

(8) Regulations for trade including Customs were developed.

(9) And indemnities were promised.

Last Days in India 1843–1850: Madras and Bangalore

Letter copied out by fond Mama with the following inscription:-

"A few extracts from my dear son's letter dated Madras, Feb. 22nd, arrived in England April 13, 1843, not quite two months, so very quick a passage. – Wonderful."

(The sheets were sewn together.)

Madras,
Feb. 22nd, 1843.

On the 20th of December we bade adieu to China. We passed Xmas Day at sea, when of course I remembered you all, and arrived at Singapore the last day of the year, and after a few days delay there to replenish our food and water, we ran up the beautiful Straits of Malacca, and with a splendid breeze soon got into the Bay of Bengal. On the 16th, after a most unprecedented passage we arrived at Madras, landed the same evening and marched to the Mount, after having been three months short of three years away from India.

We were received most cordially on our arrival at Madras, and there has been nothing going on here since we arrived but Balls and Parties to the Chinamen. I have been highly complimented on my services in China, and on our gallant Colonel (Montgomerie) being offered four appointments for disposal, he very handsomely sent for me and gave me the second choice. It was some time before I could decide whether I would continue in an appointment similar to that I held in China, or take the Horse Artillery; but though the former, as far as pecuniary advantage goes, is much the best, I preferred the Horse Artillery as I should be more the master of my own time. So I accepted the H.A. (which is looked upon in India as far superior to all the Hussars and Lancers put together).

Colonel Montgomerie, who has always been such a kind friend to me, came forward and presented me with accoutrements to the value of 1,000 Rupees. The pay is £120 a year more than the Foot Artillery, but the expenses in every way are far greater.

I am now staying at Col. Montgomerie's at Madras, fitting myself with uniform etc., preparatory to my joining the Headquarters of the Regiment now at Bangalore. The Drill of a mounted officer is much more severe than that of the Foot, however I hope six months hard work will carry me through. I have met with so much warmth and kindness from my old friends here, that I begin to look upon India again quite as my home, although I have been a long six years away from them.

At a Ball we gave the other day I was requested to forward cards of invitation to a Mrs. and Miss Pycroft. The daughter is a lively and agreeable person enough and totally devoid of any affectation or nonsense. She came to our Ball and was in raptures with the brilliancy of what, even after Bath and its Pump Room, must have appeared magnificent to her. I have met her frequently since,[1] her brother is A.D.C. to Sir Robert Dick.

When I have been fully instructed in my Cavalry Duties at Bangalore, I shall march from thence to a place called Kamptee, a distance of 700 miles, to join my Troop there stationed. Captain Amsinck, whom I frequently mentioned at Secunderabad, is one of my best friends and will be my Commanding Officer. His wife is a very nice person also and I am looking forward with a great deal of pleasure to joining them, though the station itself is not looked upon as a very healthy or agreeable one. In case I am taken sick I shall have to march 500 miles before I can reach the sea in any direction.

Fancy my having £200 worth of horseflesh, my two chargers cost me £60 each from the Government stud, they are both very fine horses and worth half as much again as the cost, I had the choice of 100 at contract price. Besides them I have a good hack which I knock about on at all times and a pegu (Burmese) pony, the first costing me £50 and the last £25.

My direction will in future be Lt. W. Baker,
Madras Horse Artillery,[2]
Bangalore,
E. India.

---

1. *It was no good his Mama getting excited as he did not marry till about 1850 and then t(*
   Edith Lushington, daughter of a judge. – Editor.
2. *He was very proud of at last being in the Horse Artillery. – Editor.*

The Travellers' Bungalow "Vamembaddy,"
En Route to Bangalore.
March 20th, 1843.

My dear Mother and Sisters,

I left Madras seven days ago and have now accomplished about 130 miles of my journey to Bangalore. Our rate of travelling with your steam notions may appear exceedingly slow, but awkward bullock carts are not great inducements for hurrying, and 16 or 17 miles a day is as much as an invalid officer with me can undergo.

On our way hither we passed through a very interesting country and the neighbourhood of Ancah and Vellone, celebrated for many hard contested struggles between Tipoo and ourselves, also the scene of that fearful Mutiny of the native Troops in 1800. I was lucky enough to be accompanied in my researches by one of the actual survivors of the Mutiny, an old Pensioner of H.M.'s 19th Dragoons who pointed out everything of interest connected with that fearful night. I also had the garrison order book of the very day to refer to, which fully showed how little suspicion the authorities had of the design about to be put into execution. The usual every day details of funds are enumerated, nothing else; those of the following are written in a hurried manner and in a new hand and refer to the immediate necessity of burying their fallen comrades, amounting to 900 principally Europeans.

I found some entertainment here also in conversing with a very aged native who said he was 120 years old, who had served under Tipoo when he beseiged this fort, and pointed out where the breach had been effected in the walls. I never saw a man with such a surprising recollection of dates, he was quite conversant with events which went back to 1760.

The alligators in the fort ditch were very large and very numerous, and were originally put there to prevent prisoners attempting to swim across.

A particular lady friend of mine has just died of cholera after only a few days' illness, the last time I had seen her she was leading off a Ball – this is continually the case in India. The Comet has excited a good deal of astonishment and the natives attribute to it all their cholera and misfortunes.

I send a Bill of Lading for the two boxes of Tea which I mentioned having sent you; George will I am sure arrange everything through his agents in London, but it is an understood thing with my agents at Madras that the tea is to be deposited at my Mother's door free of all expense whatsoever, and I hope it may be worthy of acceptance.

Bangalore,
April 23rd, 1843.

It is now just a month since I arrived at this station, having completed my march on the 26th. We are 200 or 300 feet above the level of the sea, the air is always cool and refreshing and although the sun's power is now great, the heat is by no means so oppressive as at Madras or any station that I have been at in India. I feel here less langour and fatigue, though it is the hot season, that I can recollect doing since leaving England, except for the winter in China.

Many of your English fruits flourish here, such as strawberries and apples, and this is almost the only place that I am aware of where the potato thrives.

The society here is far too large a one to please me, there being upwards of 70 visitable families residing here, exclusive of bachelors who perhaps double that number.

The Military Force here is very considerable though not equal to what I was used to at Secunderabad, in all about 6,500 fighting men, and on a Field Day I assure you, it is a sight seldom equalled by any of the grand reviews in England.

Our own party at our Mess amounts to about 20 officers. Once a fortnight we give a Ladies' Party, when those we are intimate with come to dinner and in the evening there is a dance or music. We are the only Mess that even attempts anything of the kind, these parties are therefore very popular amongst the fair sex, and as none but the first society are asked, the invitations are much sought after.

Besides riding, which has lately been rather painful owing to my trying to learn the military style and the uncomfortable position we are compelled to adopt – however I hope I shall get gradually broken in as others have done before me. Every morning an hour is employed in learning a new cavalry sword drill, and we are obliged to be present for an hour at the stables to see the horses groomed and fed and properly looked after. I found on arrival here that there was little to be done in the middle of the day, so I purchased a cheap horse and gig; this makes me keep four horses and a pony which I know you will consider very extravagant.

We are all much gratified with the Duke's speech on the thanks of Parliament being voted to the China warriors, but I wish they would give us more substantial proof of their country's approbation in the form of Prize Money.

If an opportunity offers I wish you would send me out three tortoiseshell eye-glasses No. 5. and a couple of good pen-knives[1] of Salisbury cutlery. Your chests of tea will be arriving about the time you get this.

Bangalore,
August 14th,1843.

I have seldom that I can remember, experienced more real pleasure than I did on the 16th ultimo, when it was my peculiar good fortune to receive letters from nearly every member of the family. (He here enumerates the dates of the several letters.) The intelligence lately communicated which gave me most satisfaction was Isabella's safe confinement and improved state of health. Isabella some time ago paid me the high compliment of asking me to be Godpapa, and of course a request of this nature can hardly be denied.

The Doctors have taken me in hand saying my liver has not been performing its functions properly and I am suffering from extreme debility, headaches, loss of appetite etc. and shall go for a change of air up to the hills if I do not improve. Luckily I have plenty of kind friends and good servants.

Somebody you say has been telling you that I am much grown – don't you believe any of their nonsense. I am 5 feet 11¾ inches in height and was in China 11 stone 12 pounds; now about 10 stone 8 pounds in weight. Your informant has rather exaggerated regarding the gaiety and expense of my new uniform. It is a serviceable handsome dress enough, but I am glad to say I can go to Parade in full dress for £200, which she said my jacket cost alone.

Bellary,
January 21st, 1844.

After several days I at last got off on the 29th from Bangalore. I was more sorry to leave my friends there than I have been since leaving you in 1837. Some of my most intimate friends gave me parties and Balls, but nothing flattered me so much as being escorted on my first march (11 miles) by

---

1. *It seems that pen-knives were one of our exports just then as the Chinese mentioned them also – Editor.*

several of the fair ladies of the place, and though they were all engaged to go to a Ball in the evening at Bangalore, and had been up all the previous night at one in honour of myself, they continued to camp with me all the day.

Mrs. Bighorn insisted on giving the entertainment on this occasion and for this purpose she had sent out a very large collection of tents and everything that could possibly be required in the way of eatables and drinkables. About 20 of my friends, ladies and gentlemen composed the party, and after partaking of an excellent breakfast and tiffin, with lots of fun in the interim (somewhat after the style of a picnic in England except that the sun kept us to the tents), the sun's disappearance was a signal for the ladies to resume their riding habits and take their leave of me, and heartily sorry was I to bid many of them "Adieu," as you may suppose.

I have been journeying on since then very comfortably and find the novelty of marching agrees with me far better than the monotony of garrison life, notwithstanding its gaieties and many other recommendations.

Bellary is rather a small station, there being only two Regiments and two Companies of Artillery here, but I scarcely ever met such a hospitable set of people, and during my short halt there has been one continual round of feasting. As a station it is considered hot in the extreme and hardly ever free from cholera, but luckily just now remarkably healthy.

From Camp Capadoo,
On the Bank of the Burmah River.
Feb. 17th, 1844.

I will now give you a short outline of my way of life whilst on the march.

Yesterday, knowing we had a long march the following day, the Doctor and myself turned in about 8 o'clock, giving direction to be woken at 3 a.m. Accordingly at 3 a.m., the Sergeant reports that the guard and everything has gone right during the night. It takes me half an hour to prepare for the saddle, during which time the men are similarly employed, some giving their horses their feed and the remainder striking their tents. By the time all this is done my servant has supplied me with a warm cup of ginger tea which I always take the first thing in the morning, with a biscuit, and my tent comes to the ground as I put my foot into the stirrup. The camels are loaded, two coolies start off carrying my bed, and the ground being clear of everything, I give the word of command and we move off.

Unless we have a moon it is dark for the next two or three hours and just now quite cold, and dreary enough it is, marching along only at a walking pace till the sun makes its appearance. The guide proceeds with a torch to show us the road, and as he only goes from his own village to the next, of course knows the way thoroughly. There are no hedges or land-marks, but it is not half so bad as a thick jungle, where you even lose the benefit of the stars, and have to trust entirely to your guide's local knowledge.

If all goes well, by eight o'clock we have arrived at our new ground. The person whom I have sent on in advance has selected a nice open piece of ground clear of the village and to windward of it, which I may tell you is a point of some importance to persons of acute senses! The village I hear is small but will afford us all that we require, namely milk for ourselves and grain for our horses and the river with water, and everything else we have with us. I am provided with one very good tent, 14 feet square in the clear, with a verandah all round 32 feet, and as is usual jobs with all tents in this country, they have two roofs, each of three or four cloths in thickness. You must know that the Doctor and I take it by turns to send on a tent over night and I have the satisfaction of seeing mine already pitched and my cook underneath a bank cooking, so that we don't despair of getting something for breakfast very shortly. For the next hour after coming to the ground it is a lively scene enough as we see all our things gradually coming up, and I employ myself in directing the sites for the mens' tents, and seeing the horses cleaned and fed. (Horses of course are kept in the open air and secured by pickets by the hind feet.) The Doctor sends to tell me breakfast is on the table, and with a right good appetite I proceed to examine what they've got. First there's a hare stew killed by the Doctor himself yesterday, a grilled fowl, eggs, with tea and coffee as much as we will. After bestowing half an hour on these good things, we shoulder our guns and if we have any luck, in an hour or so's walk, return with a couple or two of hares and as many partridges, sufficient indeed for dinner and the next morning's breakfast. On coming home a thorough change becomes necessary and with it a good wash which completely revives one. The thermometer is now perhaps at a 100° with such a nasty wind blowing and a cloud of dust penetrating everything. I then employ myself as I am now doing, or read till half past three, when the servant tells me I must give up the use of the table, as he wants to prepare it for dinner, and by four o'clock, a really good dinner is awaiting me of muligatawny, roast fowl, partridge pie, curry etc., no sweets of course, or vegetables as potatoes won't keep. Three glasses of beer and two of wine make up my allowance and by that time I find the sun has lost some of its power and we feel inclined for a stroll. At half past six a cup of tea and half a glass of brandy and water with a cigar, and at eight we turn in, which concludes the day.

This is not a good sporting country there being no cover for game, but we see herds of antelope every morning though they are too wild for our coming with a shot.

I have now merely mentioned what concerns my own doings but I have many troubles connected with Detachment which I shall sum up in a few words, by telling you that they are mostly raw Irishmen whose delight is to be in trouble and the country abounds with intoxicating liquors, which renders them at times very difficult to manage. In garrison, of course, guard-rooms are made strong enough to retain the most refractory in order, but here I have no such conveniences for them, and at times they occasion me a great deal of anxiety and trouble. One man I shall try by Court Martial at Sholapore and I trust 100 lashes (which is the punishment) he will receive; I think this will be a warning to the other bad ones. Cholera has been another source of anxiety to me, as we had hardly left Bellary 24 hours, when a case made its appearance in our camp and I regret to say terminated fatally. Cholera seldom makes a solitary visit of this kind, and the Doctor and myself felt considerably alarmed lest it should spread, but though many cases similar to cholera in their first symptoms followed, none of them I rejoice to say turned out seriously.

Another annoyance is the constant breaking down of our country carts which carry all the things, and we are compelled to put up with temporary repairs which are only likely to stand for a day or two.

We saw the Ruins of the celebrated city of Bijapur, now literally a city of the dead, as nought remains of its grandeur but the tombs of the kings. Amongst other sights there – which could hardly escape an Artilleryman's notice – were some most gigantic guns, which surpassed all that I had ever heard of in bulk. One made of iron was 38 feet long and six feet in circumference at the muzzle. The cockney wonders in St. James' Park are mere Popguns in comparison with these, and how and where they were constructed I am at a loss to conceive.

When I reach Sholapore I shall have completed just 420 miles of my march and go on 180 miles further with the men, and then I shall have to pursue my journey without the Doctor and I shall not want to take my leave of him as he has been a very pleasant companion.

I cannot thank you all sufficiently for the very great pleasure and entertainment your letters always afford me.

Kamptee, Central India.
Xmas Day, 1844.

To my dear mother and sisters,

I don't think I can better commence a short letter to you than by wishing you all most sincerely "A Merry Christmas" and a happy New Year, and hope there may be many more of them in store for you, though we have done this for many a year to no avail – who knows what 1845 may bring forth.

You may well say that ladies who have resided out here are indolent and enervated and ill-suited to English habits afterwards, such I am sorry to say is too frequently the case with the sex generally who come out here; but how can you expect otherwise, when half the matches that are made are merely for good looks and perhaps after only a few hours knowledge of each other.

Fortunately I was disappointed myself soon after my first arrival in the country and I have seen quite sufficient since of these unhappy early marriages to determine me not being so rash again. A pretty face may go a great way, but I shall not risk my happiness in after life on such a frail tenure.

We all meet to-day at our Company Offices where we all dine together after the old English fashion, some 20 in number, and on New Year's Day we all re-assemble again, and as we all wear Blue Jackets we try and pretend we are all one family. "Absent Friends," is the invariable toast on these occasions, so you may depend on being remembered. Our soldiers and their wives also dine together to-day. My last Xmas dinner in England was also eight years ago!

Kamptee, Central India.
June 12, 1845.

I have much pleasure in informing you of the safe arrival of the little Case which reached me in two months. The little remembrances which it contained from you all I esteemed most dear and as for the chain[1] I am quite delighted with it. It is quite the neatest and prettiest one I have ever seen of its kind and as it comprises the hair of both my parents I value it the more on that account, so now I no longer regret the loss of the other. My fair friends

---

1. *This chain was made at his request from the hair of his eight sisters and his parents and was a much treasured possession. It is quite remarkable how closely the ten specimens resemble each other.*

who have seen it admire it tremendously and appear somewhat astonished that none of you possess the same beautiful coloured Hair[1] as myself, and certainly you are very much to be pitied. Perhaps in the course of the next 15 years we shall more closely resemble each other, though possibly the advantage then may be seen still more in my favour as Red is said to be a very durable colour!

It would afford me great pleasure if my Mother could favour me with her "daguerreotype" as I believe they can be made for a trifling expense.

We had a delightful fall of rain yesterday, so that we may almost regard the worst of the hot season terminated as after the first good shower the hot winds cease, the atmosphere seems relieved of its burthen and the whole face of nature seems refreshed.

I am sitting to-day with all my windows and doors thrown open after having kept them closed for the two months previous and I feel as buoyant and well as if I had just taken a fresh lease of life.

October 10th, 1847.

(Beginning of this letter was lost.)

Since I last wrote to you I have received a special mark of H.M.'s favour, the Medal for China,[2] which had been long expected. The affair was rather an imposing one and to a person of my bashful and retiring nature, I was made rather too much of to be pleasant.

The whole force was paraded on the occasion in Full Dress, and being the only Officer to be decorated at the time, it was my singular good fortune to be addressed in very flattering terms in front of 5,000 men under arms, who afterwards saluted in a very becoming military fashion, and the whole thing went off in smoke.

I tried to persuade the Brigadier to give me a Ball on the occasion, but my impudence was no match for his avarice, though my suggestion was warmly supported by many of my lady friends!

---

1. *He had red hair!*
2 *When we remember how conceited he was about his red hair, I should say he was full of good qualities, but modesty was not one of them, but he doubtless mentioned this to please his mother. – Editor.*

Kamptee,
March 28th, 1849.

The last letter I despatched to you was penned amidst the bustle and confusion consequent upon an immediate march, for which I was completely unprepared.

A claimant to the throne of Nagpur, having collected a considerable force, had taken up his position in an old fort and threatened mischief.

I have now the pleasure to inform you of my safe return in high health and spirits after a rather laborious, but other-wise an exceedingly agreeable excursion. We were away a month and surprised the rebels who had actually invaded the Rajah's territory and in a skirmish with some of his troops gained a partial advantage. We pushed along at an astonishing pace, the Infantry making forced marches morning and evening, to enable them to keep up with the mounted portion of the Detachment. In four days we accomplished nigh 100 miles, which to your Railway notions may appear no great undertaking, but you must bear in mind the nature of the roads in this country, the heat, and that we had to carry every sort of necessity with us, only excepting water, which was not always plentiful, so it may be accounted good marching. On more than one occasion my men were from 10 to 11 hours in the saddle, but though fatigued of course, not a man or a horse fell sick. After a few days I found that very few could stand what I could, which I attribute to the regular horse exercise and rackets which I am accustomed to, combined with something of an iron constitution. Notwithstanding the rapidity of our movements however, the insurgents were always forewarned of our approach, and conceiving discretion the better part of valour, disbanded themselves over the country, so with the exception of 120 which we took by surprise and made prisoners, after scouring the country and stirring up their old haunts without success, we retraced our steps to this station at our leisure.

You must know that this Troop has acquired rather an unenviable reputation of late, chiefly from drinking. Harsh treatment, combined with want of tact towards the men has been productive of discontent and bad conduct on their part. I had always stood their friend which they knew, so on assuming charge I appealed to their better feelings and told them I should deem it a proof of their good will towards me if they would conduct themselves properly, and I had the extreme gratification of returning to this station without finding the slightest fault. I have since been complimented on the state of efficiency of Horse and Foot Artillery, both being under my command and mustering four guns altogether.

On the morning of our return I had a good substantial cold collation with beer etc. prepared for them, of which many of them partook with their wives and 100 others were married, so that we wound up mutually satisfied.

Having excellent servants and sparing no expense on the march, I fared admirably the whole time, and always had my tents up in good time. Some of our night marches were rather wearisome as, starting as we did at midnight, or soon after, we trudged along for five or six hours in darkness. However, the men broke into good old English Glees and Choruses as we went along, and there being many excellent singers amongst them, it relieved us amazingly in a thick jungle full of wild brutes on either side of the path. The horses were wonderful at finding their way in the darkness; the singers would strike up "Home, sweet Home," or "That old House at Home" which was a great favourite with them and 25 voices would immediately take it up. The effect in the stillness which enveloped us was most soothing and many a time my thoughts have wandered back to the Wylye drawing-room and its tenants of former days.

We are expecting to hear Lord Gough's recall on the news of the Battle of Chillianwallah reaching England. He is a fine, gallant old soldier but even when opposed to such an inferior army as the Chinese proved himself no General.

The Governor-General is in a dilemma now as to the disposal of the country, the annexation of the Punjab being warmly advocated by all Indians.

The thermometer was 110° in my tent the other day but I was so busily engaged I cared little about it.

Kamptee,
December 10th, 1849.

We have just got through our Review and Annual Inspection (the most tiresome season of the year) with some élat; the Troops acquitted themselves most satisfactorily.

The fine, bracing, cold season has again returned to us, and the reign of sickness, cholera and all its terrors seems for the present to have come to a close. By the middle of March the hot weather will have commenced again, and from that time till November, heat, rains and sickness follow each other in quick succession. This year the mortality has been unusual and our small body (only 110 or so) has suffered considerably.

A vast number of Corps are in motion just now as a general relief in Bengal is taking place, and many of our Madras Regiments are occupying stations up there. A considerable portion of this Force have already taken their departure and the place is consequently immensely dull and desolate and will continue so until the new Regiments arrive. I was particularly intimate with one family called Woomer and spent many agreeable hours with them. Now, alas, they have gone, and perhaps during the whole of my servitude we may never cross each other again – such is Indian Society.

It is fortunate these marches are not of frequent occurrence, as to a poor man it is utter ruination. Now for instance when I came here I made myself very cosy and comfortable and furnished the house very neatly; indeed some ladies who did me the honour of dining with me the other day, assured me that I was far too comfortable for a bachelor; however that may be the things are now all on my hands, and I shall have to sell them at a great sacrifice or leave them to the newcomers at their own valuation, but £100 will re-furnish any house almost.

I give the men and their wives and families an entertainment at the end of next week, when a bullock and some 10 sheep will be slaughtered for the occasion, to be washed down with a bottle of Beer per man, and a bottle of Milk Punch for each of their wives, and a supper after the Ball.

I shall hold command now to Bangalore, whither I shall arrive about the end of March.

Bangalore,
April 25th, 1850.

To his dear mother and sisters,

We had hardly entered on our Xmas festivities when we were amazed on the receipt of a peremptory order, directing us to march out of Kamptee on the morning of New Year's Day, and from that time up to a week or 10 days ago, I have never known what it was to have a moment's leisure. My bungalow was soon converted into a barn as I parted with all my things at nearly the prices I paid for them six years ago, a proof of purchasing good articles. There were hundreds of persons thronging about my place, morning, noon and night, as the innumerable marching followers have usually to be engaged by the Commanding Officer, and it is his duty to inspect all the cattle required, also the carts, coolies, and to see agreements signed. Advances have to be paid to all these people and then I have all our Mess arrangements to make, there being no one else to do the thankless office of Caterer.

Besides all this fatigue we have to do the polite [thing] at endless farewell parties, which were intended kindly, but to my thinking were monstrous inconvenient. However, I found on being about to quit that I was parting with half a dozen very kind sincere friends that I should find a difficulty elsewhere in replacing. But the best friends must part, so after seeing the New Year in at a Ball, and having our healths drunk in due form by the party, I sought an opportunity of slipping away unperceived to get a couple of hours sleep. About an hour before daylight, the Brigade, Troop and Horse Artillery were in motion to the southward, and after being stationed at Kamptee nearly 12 years, out of the 120 original men, only five were left to accompany the Regiment down country. After a short dissertation to the men from me and a cheer for the friends we left behind, away we went.

The whole of the Nizam's country was in a state of anarchy and confusion, but we miraculously managed to avoid bloodshed.

The road we traversed had not been travelled by guns for 20 years, and it is only for four or five months in the year that parties are permitted to proceed by it, as a very bad fever prevails in the normal Jungles, added to which the passes are so bad, that another road is preferred though 100 miles further round. For nearly 30 miles it was nothing but a dense forest full of every description of wild beast. The road has about 30 yards of clearance as the underwood is burnt periodically. The second day after we left, heavy rains set in which rendered the road wholly impassable, so I pulled up for two days and a pretty mess we were in, tents blown down, dozens of horses loose at a time, galloping about and frightening day and night, but fortunately no serious injury was done. At length it cleared up and we proceeded on our journey, but the rain stuck closely to us all the way down to Secunderabad, which added much to our troubles.

I met with great attention at Secunderabad and found many old friends; from thence to Kurnoul a distance of about 140 miles. My troubles continued as the whole of the country abounds in intoxicating liquors, and notwithstanding all my exertions the men got hold of it and I had difficulty in keeping them in order and had to try another man by Court Martial, after which my troubles on this score ceased.

After numerous upsets we got through the passes without any serious accidents, tho' we had some narrow escapes. On one occasion the six horses were unable to make way with the gun at a very steep slope, the footing being very slippery. At last they lost ground, and the whole mass, horses guns, men etc. – after acquiring considerable velocity – went over bodily backwards. I thought neither man nor horse could have survived it, but they were not even badly bruised. I have often thought that our men bear charmed lives.

The rivers gave us some heavy work – one was three quarters of a mile across, but we managed to get across and reached Secunderabad in six weeks from Kamptee. Up to this time the men had worked like horses, but on reaching that station they encountered some old ship mates and broke loose, and I had to make a severe example of two by another Court Martial. I stopped four days and had to draw all the pay, a most complicated business, then to get the guns and carriages repaired at the Arsenal, to lay in all sorts of fresh supplies and change all our carts and coolies etc., I used to go to bed completely tired out and not get a wink of sleep in consequence of such vast anxiety.

From Kurnoul[1] to Bangalore, the last 70 miles of roads are as good as the old turnpikes in England. As we began to approach Bangalore I began to feel nervous as to the reception I should meet with, as the General commanding there is a great martinet, and keeps all under him in a constant state of alarm and fidget. I halted therefore a day to brush up before we marched in, and I wrote to Adey to come out and see me which he accordingly did, and I since have seen a good deal of him and like him very much. He is younger than I am and very fond of the polka and that sort of thing, which I begin to feel too antiquated to take part in.

On the morning of the 30th of March we entered this station, and at the outskirts of the Cantonment I was met by appointment, by the much-dreaded General and his Staff. He casually inspected us, put numerous questions to me connected with the march and seemed very well satisfied. He expressed himself well pleased with the high condition and appearance of the horses and men, and congratulated me on making such a very successful march, not having lost man, woman or child, followers or horses, throughout the whole distance of 700 miles in camp; a thing unparalleled, when you consider that I must have had nigh 1,000 souls and 150 Troopers with the Camp. I marched in without a sick man and only three or four sick horses, so my good fortune was extraordinary. Our own Colonel, a man of few words, has been most lavish in his praise, so that instead of censure

---

1.   *A gun taken at the Siege of Kurnoul is now in the R.M.A. grounds at Sandhurst. – Editor*

and abuse which I expected, I have been most agreeably surprised. So having brought my march to a happy termination and after discharging various accounts etc., I now feel myself quite a free man and I hope I shall have a year or two of peace and quietness.

I have now got a very comfortable bungalow and am busy making myself snug, as we shall in most likelihood be here for four or five years, that is if all remains quiet and no outbreaks. I am now nearer to you than I was at Kamptee. We have a carriage going daily to the beautiful Nilgiri Hills, so we are only two days removed from an English climate. We have strawberries and English vegetables here, such as peas and potatoes in abundance, and such a treat they are after being accustomed to no other vegetables, but those we had in tins from England, hermetically sealed. My pay here is considerably reduced, as Bangalore is much more expensive than Kamptee, but the necessaries of life are much cheaper and 50 other things reconcile me to the change.

We have been fêted by all the Regiments on our arrival here and I have made more of than I ever was before, enjoying the place of honour and having healths drunk and all that sort of thing.

And now my dear Mother, with every good wish,
Your affectionate son,
Wyndham Baker.

Postscript

It was sad that at Mrs. Widdicombe's death, my top copy of Wyndham's letters was lost. I had lent them her to read in print. My second copy was not quite complete, and lacked the last letter of all, which told of the arrival of Wyndham's bride from England, with her trousseau and many trunks and all the excitement. When one remembers that he took out five dozen shirts, one can imagine how vast her trousseau might have been.

I am sorry too that this last letter was lost, as it always seemed to me a very fitting ending to the series, with our hero at last finding the lady of his choice and settling down to live happily ever after!

(Col. Wyndham Baker married Edith Lushington, the daughter of a judge in the Indian Civil Service.)

Further Information

Addiscombe

When Addiscombe[1] was founded in 1809, the Royal Military Academy was taken as a model, the cadets forming an Artillery Company in blue, and wearing the same Ordnance badge.

> "With his coat faced with red and shoulder-knots bright,
> His 'bezzars too large and trousers too tight,
> His dress cap and belt quite twenty years old,
> Here's our Addiscombe lad with heart true as gold!
>
> Oh, we are the lads of the army,
> Our lass and our grog is our boast;
> But ladies, don't let me alarm you,
> Here's our Addiscombe lads for a toast!"

Sent by a cadet of 1840–42.

William Draper, a son-in-law of the celebrated John Evelyn, inherited the old house through his Aunt, Lady Temple, and started to rebuild the mansion in 1702; it was solid brick Elizabethan architecture, consisting of a basement, two elaborate state storeys and an attic. "The architect was probably Vanbrugh".

Evelyn says in his Memoirs of 11th July, 1703:

"I went to Addiscombe, 16 miles from Wotton, to see my son-in-law's new house. The outside to the covering being such excellent brickwork based with Portland stone with the pilasters, windows and within, that I pronounced it in all points of solid and good architecture to be one of the very best gentleman's houses in Surrey when finished."

1. *From "Addiscombe, Its Heroes and Men of Note," by Col. H.M. Vibart, kindly lent by Lt.Col. C.B. Appleby, D.S.O., F.S.A., Director, National Army Museum, Sandhurst; and from Major W. Broadfoot's article in "Blackwood's Magazine," in 1893.*

Later, it was sold in 1809 by a Mr. Radcliffe to the Hon. East India Company.

The entrance was in the east or public front by a flight of steps which led into the great hall, over the central windows of this front and above the attic was the inscription in Roman characters:

"Non faciam vitio culpave minorem."

This is probably the motto of the Drapers and may be translated, "I will not lower myself to vice or fault." To the west or garden front was a handsome brick portico or loggia. The entrance hall led to the grand staircase by which there was an ascent to the saloon which was very magnificent. The walls and ceilings of the grand staircase and saloon were decorated with paintings from the heathen mythology, chiefly by Sir James Thornhill, and finished in a masterly manner. The circular compartment of the ceiling represented the Feast of Bacchus... There were five doors leading out of the saloon over which were as many allegorical subjects, such as Diana visiting Endymion sleeping, Danae and the golden shower, Britannia leading the Goddess of Justice by the hand, Pan surprising the nymph Syrinx, and Flora reclining against Zephyrus; while the arms of the East India Company were over the fireplace.

History does not relate what the first cadets thought of it all and it seems a great pity that no one recorded their comments!

Major Broadfoot in his paper on Addiscombe in Blackwood's Magazine of May, 1893, states that the mansion was whitewashed. If so, it could only have been done outside, where it was less important as a sanitary precaution, as inside, the painted walls still remained. Major Broadfoot suggests that it was perhaps considered necessary to purify the house after the departure of Lord Liverpool and his friends, Pitt and Dundas, before it was fit for the education of youthful and innocent cadets!

Several stories are told of the lively frolics of statesmen of the highest rank within its walls. On one occasion, it is related that Pitt, wishing to return to London in the early hours of the morning, galloped through the toll-gate without paying the toll-fees, and was fired at by the disappointed and exasperated toll-keeper. On another occasion, Pitt, returning to town, lost his way, owing either to the darkness of the night, or to his having imbibed rather more champagne than was prudent, and passing somewhat noisily near a farm, was mistaken for a highwayman, and fired at by the irritated and frightened farmer. The incident is alluded to in the following lines from the Rolliad.

> "Ah! think what danger on debauch attends,
> Let Pitt, once drunk, preach temp'rance to his friends,
> How, as he wandered darkling o'er the plain,
> His reason drown'd in Jenkinson's champagne,
> A rustic's hand, but righteous fate withstood,
> Had shed a Premier's for a robber's blood."

Addiscombe House was now to be devoted to very different uses, and was no more to hear "sounds of revelry by night," except in the adjoining barracks. The use of wines, spiritous liquor and tobacco in and every precaution was enjoined on the authorities of the Seminary to keep the place free from such contraband articles.

We hear that the first regulations under which the cadets were admitted were somewhat as follows:

"Cadets must be above 14, and under 18 years. From 14-16, not under 4 ft. 9 ins. in height; and from 17-18, not under 5 ft. 2 ins.

"It was indispensable that the cadets before admission should have a fair knowledge of Arithmetic, write a good hand, and possess a competent knowledge of English and Latin grammar. They should also have learnt Drawing and have some knowledge of French, Mathematics and Fortification."

Each cadet paid £30 half-yearly to cover the cost of books, mathematical instruments, stationery, pocket-money (2/6d. a week) washing etc., "cloaths and medical attendance;" the further cost of education was paid by the Company to secure useful and efficient men for their work in India.

Public Examinations were to take place twice a year. No cadet was to be allowed to enter the Seminary with a greater sum than half a guinea in his possession, and any deviation from this rule subjected the cadet to removal from the Seminary. Masters were prohibited from taking any fee, gratuity or reward, while cadets were to conduct themselves respectfully towards Professors and Tutors and were cautioned to avoid all quarrelling, fighting and loose or improper language to one another. From 1809 to 1813 their numbers rose from 60 to 90 and were formed into three academies. By 1816 the cadets stayed two years and had to provide the following:

One military great-coat.
One uniform jacket, waistcoat & Pr. pantaloons.
One military cap & feather[1]. with plate in front embossed with the Company's arms.
Ten shirts.
Six pairs of cotton socks.
Six pairs of worsted socks.
Two pairs of gaiters.
Two pairs of military gloves.
Two pairs of strong shoes.
Six towells.
Six night-caps[1].
Six pocket handkerchiefs.
Two black silk handkerchiefs.
Two combs and a brush.
One toothbrush.
One foraging cap.

The Company supplied each cadet with the following clothing: a jacket, waistcoat, black silk handkerchief and foraging cap half-yearly; pantaloons and gaiters quarterly; and shoes every two months.

Addiscombe owned 88 acres in 1826, two thirds of which formed a farm, and about 30 acres surrounding the mansion house was used by the cadets. A new drawing and lecture hall with arcades beneath, was erected in 1821, this was the building so well-known as the "chapel". It was used for many purposes, for morning and evening prayer, for examinations, and for distribution of prizes on the Public Examination Day.

---

1. *The italics are mine. – Editor.*

In September, 1825, new buildings were erected to accomodate 150 cadets, and each cadet should have a space 9 ft. x 6 ft. in his dormitory. At a later date framed partitions were arranged so as to separate every sleeping place – these were called "kennels!"

Two additional wings, four classrooms, a new dining hall, bake-house, dairy, laundry, brew-house and other store-rooms etc., were all built by 1828 at a cost of £21,397. And in April 1825, guns and mortars were supplied by the Ordnance Dept. and in those early days there were two large brass guns in front of the mansion besides two smaller mortars.

So we can see that by the time young Wyndham Baker reached Addiscombe in 1835, it was quite a big place well established in its own grounds.

As Col. Vibart says: "It will appear from the details of the meals provided for cadets, that they were not reared in the lap of luxury!"

Breakfast.	Tea and bread and butter, or bread and milk if preferred.
Lunch.	Bread and cheese with good table beer.
Dinner.	Beef, mutton and veal alternately, of the best kind, with occasional change to pork when in season.
Tea.	With bread and butter, or bread and cheese and beer if preferred.

As we hear that the cadets and masters were to be dieted at 1s. 9d. per head, and servants at 1s. 6d., the fact that the housekeepers could only produce a sparse and monotonous diet was not so surprising, even in those cheap days.

When duelling broke out amongst the cadets, there was an enquiry and the Seminary rules were modified so as to make life more worth living and particularly to admit of indulgence in what the authorities styled the "filthy and pernicious habit of smoking!"

Jonathan Cape was appointed Senior Professor in 1822 and remained at the College for 39 years – the most remarkable master they ever had. The fees went up from £30 to £40 in 1821 – £65 for the first year and £50 for the second year in 1829 – and in 1835 the Court of Directors made the charge £240 for the two years training.

This would have been the amount young Wyndham's parents would have had to pay – rather a large sum no doubt for a struggling parson with so large a family to bring up!

The Addiscombe cadets, however, were out to make the best of a spartan life. In the early days they played their professors up with all kinds of tricks in the time honoured manner of schoolboys, and risked being given extra drill or "swat" (mathematics)! They had ways of getting out at night to forbidden pubs and used to frequent Mrs. Rose's cottage to buy food and sit in her parlour for a quiet smoke – she must have been a bit of a mother to them.

There is a lovely story of a window whose iron bars had been broken and were mended by day with black putty. This made a convenient way of escape. Once when there was nearly a fire in the middle of the night, the cadets put out the fire, and the local press got hold of the story, which made the governors sit up and wonder how on earth the cadets had managed to escape, as they were firmly locked up in their barracks each night by the sergeant who kept the key when he put the lights out at 10 p.m. After this there was a terrific search by the authorities, but they failed to detect the black putty bars! At another time when the governors were due to celebrate some occasion with a cold banquet in the Great Hall, some enterprising brave spark managed to whisk away an entire cold turkey with all its trimmings to provide a midnight feast for the cadets. However, they were lucky that time too and were saved by a friendly sergeant.

There was always football and it seems to have been a game played with no rules as regards numbers or anything else, a cross between soccer, rugger and the Eton Wall-game. At any rate a player could run with the ball until he was tripped up, and then the other players in their efforts to extract the ball, piled themselves on top of him, a kicking, struggling mass known as a "rosh;" this went on until someone managed to get the ball clear and throw it to one of his own side or take it on himself. The daily game was "Old and Young Cadets" v. "Browns and Greens." The seniors always took advantage of the best goal and kicked downhill, but their number was always far less than their opponents.

The great matches of the year were Browns v. Greens; Young

Cadets v. Browns and Greens; and Old Cadets v. Young Cadets.

Cadets in the first, second, third and fourth terms were styled Greens, Browns, Young Cadets and Old Cadets respectively, and to each were attached certain obligations. The Young and Old cadets were the privileged classes and made a set of rules which the new boys had to follow, rather like our public schoolboys of to-day.

One such rule was not to smoke in the vicinity outside the College, except at the "Corner," i.e. the sunny side of Lord Ashburton's garden wall, in the high road from Addiscombe to Addington.

Another was "not to carry their gloves under their shoulder straps," a privilege reserved for Young and Old cadets.

And lastly, not to go to Mother Rose's cottage on their personal business, but only whilst fetching anything for an Old or Young cadet.

The Hong Merchants, the Factories and Pidgin-English

The Co-Hong was said to be the milker of foreign trade, milking it all it could stand, but for this privilege it also paid heavily. The position of the Hong merchants was undoubtedly very profitable, though their losses were occasionally large and the "squeezes" almost without end, their purses being emptied for such things as famine relief, flood damage or the erection of municipal buildings; from the length and breadth of the great Empire of China, calls came in upon the Hong merchants.

Hunter, in his "Fan Kwae at Canton", declares that a licence paid to Peking by a Hong merchant could amount to as much as £55,000 sterling; whilst Basil Lubbock tells us that in 1841, when the burden of ransoming Canton from the troops of Sir Hugh Gough, fell chiefly upon the Hong merchants, Howqua gave 1,100,000 dollars, Pwankeiqua 260,000; and the rest of the co-Hong 640,000 dollars. He also says that this was not the only time that poor Howqua paid out a million. However, we hear, that in spite of all this, when he valued his fortune in 1834, it was 26 million dollars, about five million odd sterling – quite a considerable fortune for those days.

The Factories were built by the Hong merchants on the banks of the Pearl River, opposite the great city of Canton facing south, they were 10 miles from the Whampoa Anchorage, 40 miles from the Bogue Forts, 60 miles from Lintin and 80 miles from Macao.

It was the only piece of Chinese ground where a foreigner was safe before the First Opium War, and even this was due to the good offices of the Hong merchants. They were not only held responsible for every foreigner in Canton, but for every ship at Whampoa, the port of Canton. It was through them that the Hoppo or Mandarin of the Customs received all payments of duty.

To give an illustration of the extent to which the early foreign merchants were bullied, we need only look at the list of some of the Regulations laid down for the control of the foreigner, given in "Far Eastern International Relations," by Morse and MacNair.

2) "Women[1] must not be brought to the Factories"; nor could guns spears or other arms. This rule was rigorously enforced. As late as 1830 the Chinese twice threatened to stop the trade, in order to enforce the immediate departure of ladies who had come from Macao to visit the Factories.

5) "Foreigners must not use sedan chairs". Walking was the only mode of progression suitable for such folk as the foreign traders, and not too much of that.

6) "Foreigners must not row for pleasure on the river". Three days in the month they might take the air at Fati, the flower gardens across the river, in small parties, under the escort of an interpreter, who was held, literally and personally responsible for all their misdeeds. This rule was generally relaxed, but frequent efforts were made to tighten the reigns. There was, however, no relaxation as to walking through the streets even in the vicinity of the Factories.

When one remembers that the space for promenading in front of the Factories was about 1,100 feet in length with a general depth of 700 feet, the poor merchants did not have much room for exercise. In

---

1. *It is amusing to see that women were classed with guns and spears! – Editor.*

fact, when news of one of the earliest engagements was announced, and the pair were married at Canton, people lifted their eyebrows and wondered where the young hopefuls had managed to do their wooing!

As the business of a merchant was very much looked down on in China, the great Hong merchants purchased Mandarin's rank in order to maintain their dignity. Mandarins were people having authority, some sort of government official, the grade being noted by the colour of the button worn on a Mandarin's cap. The grade purchased by the Hong merchants was as a rule that of the "blue button."

Mr. Chang, in his book "Commissioner Lin and the Opium War", tells us that Pidgin-English is a singular admixture of corrupted Portuguese, English, Hindustani, and other foreign words spoken largely in a Chinese syntax. The word pidgin itself is a corruption of the English word "business". Words of Portuguese origin include such jargon as "mandarin," from *mandarim*, derived from the Malay word *mantri* (minister of state); and the Portuguese word *mandar* (to order); "compradore," from *compra* (to buy); "grand," from *grande* (the chief); "junk," from *junco* which has a Javanese origin. "Shroff," (money-dealer), and "coolie" (labourer), are words borrowed from Arabic and Hindustani respectively.

Smug Boats

From "The Opium Clippers" by Basil Lubbock

"The smug boats had, as a rule, from sixty to seventy oarsmen, sitting like galley slaves on low benches, ranged along the deck on either side. There is no finer boatman in the world than the Canton Chinaman, who besides being most enduring and incredibly active was a very skilled waterman and uncannily intelligent. The smugglers' boats, however, did not entirely depend on their oars, but had large "mat and rattan" fore and main sails. Besides being of great length, the smug boats were beamy, and broadened out in the stern so as to provide living quarters for the brokers' agents. They were, of course, well armed with cannon of sorts in the bow, swivels along each rail, and a motley armament of spears, swords, cuirasses and flintlock muskets.

"The weapons were ostensibly for use against pirates, who swarmed outside the Bocca, but there was many an occasion when a "scrambling dragon" came off best in a running fight with an "Imperial dragon.""

Musselshell Boats
From "The Chinese Repository"

In 1832, the "Chinese Repository"[1] reported that piracy was prevalent in some parts of Canton Province. The thieves had devised a new type of boat carrying 60 to 70 men, called "musselshell boats", in contrast to the older and very common "crab-boats". Having amassed 20 of these craft, the pirates captured wealthy citizens and held them for ransom. When they even dug up graves and plundered them for clothes by daylight, the Imperial anger was aroused, and the Emperor's Edict said:

"What are the local officers attending to? Why do they sit like wooden idols and suffer such bold-faced unfearing wickedness? Let Le and Choo command severely all their subordinates to exert themselves sincerely and bring to strict punishment every pirate that exists, till not one is left to slip out of the net. Thus shall cruelty be eradicated and the spirit of perverseness be torn up."

Compradores, Supercargoes, Shroffs, and Canton – A City of Boats
From "The Opium Clippers" by Basil Lubbock.

"Besides the linguists on the ships who acted as buffers between the sailors and the natives, the most important person to the tea and

---

1. *"The Chinese Repository" was the first English newspaper in China produced with the help of young Matheson.*

opium trade, was the all-important compradore, who acted as chief clerk, head of the office, cashier and custodian of the Treasury, besides confidential and private secretary to the Taipan of the Factory, even arranging his meals.

"The Purser and Supercargoes of the ships were dependent greatly on the compradore and his shroffs (clerks). Even a small coaster carried two shroffs. Their chief duty was to test the silver, whether it happened to be in coined dollars or lumps shaped like a lady's shoe, which was called 'Sycee silver'.

"The shroff, in passing a dollar as good, stamped it with his own particular sign, and if it afterwards proved to be base metal, he had to refund the amount. When ashore he usually carried a small pair of scales attached to a belt at his waist."

Basil Lubbock called Canton "a city of boats." He said: "Not only were there all kinds of queer craft, but great coasting junks all the way from Manila, Borneo, Java and Singapore, who came right up to the city and disputed place with tiers of salt-Junks from the South-West Coast.

"Then there were whole streets of shop and store boats, selling every kind of article from food to flowers, from toys to trousers. There were barbers' boats, fortune-tellers' boats, theatrical boats and palatial house-boats belonging to wealthy Chinamen. There were boats like farmyards with families of ducks swimming alongside the boats of singing birds. In and out amongst this busy throng plied the sampans and tank-boats and large ferry-boats.

"From well below Dutch Folly Fort to the landing place at Jackass Point there was no room to row and oars had to be replaced by paddles in the captains' gigs and ships' galleys which came up from the big ship anchorage in Whampoa Reach.

"Whampoa had been the harbour of Canton ever since the year 1745, when, by order of the Emperor Yung Ching, foreign vessels were not permitted further up the Canton River than Wang-Po or Yellow Anchorage.

"The actual buying and selling of opium in Chinese waters was carried on by brokers, the Hong merchants had nothing to do with the illegal trade – at any rate openly. The brokers sold the opium at Canton for cash only and orders to deliver the opium were sent to the receiving ships lying at Lintin Island by what the English called 'smug boats' and the Chinese, with their love for quaint names, called 'fast crabs' or 'scrambling dragons'!"

Cumsha.

"On delivery of the opium, the receiving ships were paid 5 dollars per chest, which was called '*cumsha*' (literally 'gold sand'), and 2 dollars for '*demurrage*' if the order was not presented within seven days."

From "The 'Fan Kwae' at Canton before Treaty Days."
1825–1844.
by William C. Hunter.

Note from Admiral Elliot

From a "Memoir of Admiral the Hon. Sir George Elliot,
written for His Children", London, H. Weede, Printed 1863.

This is a dispatch from Admiral Elliot on his retirement, trying to justify his failure to advance on Peking up the Peiho River when the Fleet was there. He had evidently been criticized at home, and it seems there was general ingnorance about the opium trade in England at that time.

He says: "I have seen remarks, (I suppose newspaper) on the impropriety of not forcing the negotiations in the north when we were once there. In the first place it was simply impossible. The anchorage to the Peiho is quite open – the cold and foul-weather monsoon was just setting in – our communication with the shore had already become difficult and doubtful, and would very shortly cease entirely, and the coast would be frozen. Even had it been otherwise, our demands for satisfaction were for what had occurred at Canton, and had assuredly never been faithfully reported to Peking. Constant reference would have therefore been necessary to Canton, and an answer could not be expected in less than three months – the ordinary post being 45 days. But it is useless to combat the remarks of people who are perfectly ignorant, not only of the main points, but of all local circumstances which often have great weight. For instance, the Chinese opium trade is talked of in England as if it was carried on by English smuggling vessels, in defiance of the Chinese custom-house authorities, whereas it is as open a trade as any other. Opium is prohibited by Imperial Decree, but every year a duty is fixed on it, and agreed to, by the importers and the Mandarins, all of which is shared between the Governor of the province and the Mandarins of various sorts.

The opium vessels lie at the islands called by the Chinese the "Outer Waters", which is beyond the control of the Custom-house officers, and there the Chinese opium boats come for what they want, tea of course, paying on the spot in dollars... They go up the rivers openly, passing closely to the Chinese forts, where occasionally they are called in and the opium chests counted, I suppose as a check on their cheating. The Chinese pay the duty, the ship importing the opium has nothing to do with that. The trade is as open as any other, and, in fact, the importing ships have nothing to do with even the authorized smuggling, if such a term can be applied to it, merely because the Government does not receive the duty levied by their own officers and paid in the same way as any other duty is paid.

If we were to prohibit the opium trade with China there would not be one chest less imported. It is a profitable trade, and foreigners would carry it on; and if you prohibit the growth of opium or its export in India, Java alone could with ease supply all China – they already grow a great deal, and could grow any quantity the market required... for all nations carry on the opium trade. I have myself seen Dutch, American, Swedish and Danish opium vessels, and there is a considerable Spanish and Portuguese trade carried on."

Lin Tse-hsu

"The Opium Clippers" by Basil Lubbock tells us quite a lot about that colourful character – Commissioner Lin! While from Mr. Chang's very scholarly work "Commissioner Lin and the Opium War", I have gathered something of his importance in Chinese history.

The first war which took place between Great Britain and the "Celestial Empire" has generally been called the Opium War, but that was far from the only cause. The Emperor and his Mandarins were very ignorant of the world outside China, and the Emperor's usual custom was to heap insults on all foreign emissaries. The British Agents showed great forbearance and were continually rebuked by Lord Palmerston, who could not visualize the state of affairs in Peking and Canton, any more than the Tao-Kuang Emperor, "the Son of Heaven", could appreciate the power and Naval might of the red-headed devils (US).

Private junks contended with mandarins' boats for the "foreign mud" (opium) in the holds of the clippers and smug boats, while the Emperor's ministers complained "that black dirt was always coming in and pure silver always going out". And this loss of specie was probably the deciding factor which induced the Emperor to appoint the implacable Commissioner Lin, with full powers to put an absolute stop to the opium trade. Another important factor was that opium smoking was rife in the Chinese armed forces. As Lin Tse-hsu's memorial said: "If we continue to pamper it [opium], a few decades from now we shall not only be without soldiers to resist the enemy, but also in want of silver to provide an army." Mr. Chang says that this was to be memorized by practically every schoolchild in the following century.

The reputation of Lin as an honest administrator was well-known throughout the "Flowery Land". Born in 1785, he was a native of Foochow in the maritime Province of Fukien, a man who had earned a high place in the Imperial favour, through not only being a great scholar and a true patriot, but a ruler who could be depended upon to overcome all opposition. He was, however, quite ignorant of the world outside China.

Lin Tse-hsu had achieved his degree (chu-jen) in 1804 and was on the secretarial staff of Chang Shih-ch'eng, the Governor of Fukien, from 1806–14, where he learnt a great deal about administering a Province. He was called "Lin Ch'ing-t'ien", or "Lin, the Clear Sky," a most coveted nickname due to his upright reputation.

Lin was promoted to the governorship of Kiangsu in 1832 where thousands gathered to greet him, the fame of his good work having gone abroad; he was known for his industry, strong desire to improve the government and his complete devotion to the welfare of the people. He was by now an expert on water conservation, flood control, social relief and tax collection, and kept this post for five years until he was made Governor of Hu-Kuang (Hupeh and Hunan) in 1837, where he stayed until the Emperor chose him to stamp out the opium trade and made him Commissioner at Canton in 1839.

Lin Tse-hsu could be said to belong to a group of progressive scholars in China who wanted reforms; he never wanted his own personal grandeur, his ambition was always for reform. He could be said to be a century ahead of his time in China, because it took the Opium War with the British to shake the Chinese Empire out of its state of ages-old lethargy and apathy with regard to the west, and start it on a slow and painful process of modernization and real trading on equal terms with the outside world.

"When he came to Canton, Lin was about 54, short and rather stout, with a keen dark eye looking out of a smooth full, round face, which except for a slender black beard, was hairless... he seldom smiled."[1] "He was carried in a sedan chair by 12 bearers and accompanied by an orderly, 6 servants and 3 cooks. His luggage was carried in 3 carts, 1,200 miles from Peking to Canton in 60 short days.

"Commissioner Lin staged his own arrival at Canton with the Viceroy... He arrived by water in a large very ornate black and gold imperial pulling-boat at 8.30 on the morning of Sunday, March 10th, 1839. This dragon led a procession of other official boats of the chop-boat description. Each boat had the rank of its occupants painted on its sides in gold letters and flew a flag in its stern. Their crews were all clad in new uniforms of red trimmed with white, and wore cone-shaped hats of rattan. His Excellency Lin, the Kin-Chae, who, it was said, had once worked as a day labourer in his father's porcelain factory, held himself with dignity, looking sternly to the front, and seated in solitary state, his nearest attendants, some red and blue button mandarins, taking care to keep their distance..."[2]

1. From "*Commissioner Lin and the Opium War*" by *Hsin-pao Chang.*
2. From "*The Opium Clippers*" by *Basil Lubbock.*

On March 17th, the Hong merchants were summoned to an audience. They went in fear and trembling, but Lin's object was to get the names of the foreign opium dealers. On the next day the Hong merchants were summoned and thoroughly frightened, being told that their heads would pay for it if the opium trade was not stopped. "No have see no fashion before," whimpered one of them. That same day Commissioner Lin issued a long edict ordering all opium to be surrendered under penalty of death. Next morning, the chief opium merchants Messrs. Matheson, Green, Dent, Daniell, Whetmore and the Parsee Dadablioy Rustomjee, met the Hong merchants to discuss what was to be done. They finally decided to offer Lin 1,034 chests of opium, out of a total of about 15,000 chests valued at 725,000 dollars. This offer, needless to say, was disdainfully refused.

Later, on March 27th, Captain Charles Elliot said he could collect 20,283 chests and delivered them up on April 10th. "Commissioner Lin[1] and the Governor of Canton proceeding to the Bogue to witness the destruction of opium in person. All the ships surrendered their opium and it was broken up and mixed with water salt and lime until it dissolved in trenches, then the liquid was made to flow through screens into a creek and from thence to the ocean."[1]

The Blockade of Canton

William C. Hunter in his "The Fan Kwae at Canton", gives an amusing account of the besieged inmates of the Factories trying to fend for themselves, when all their coolies were taken away and men in those days were not used to fending for themselves, or coping with domestic chores! This was when the Chinese blockaded the British in their Factory.

He says: "We could all clean knives, sweep floors, and even manage to fill the lamps. But there were mysteries which we could not devine; our chief, Mr. Green, after a vain attempt to boil rice – which, when prepared, resembled a tough mass of glue – proved a most wretched cook, and took to polishing the silver, but abandoned that and finally

---

1.   *From "Commissioner Lin and the Opium War" by Hsin-pao Chang.*

swept the floor! Mr. Low conscientiously did all he could, but after toasting the bread to death, and boiling the eggs till they acquired the consistency of grape-shot, he abandoned that department and took to one not exacting so much exercise of mind, and 'laid the cloth' dexterously and well. The rest of us, from modesty or feeling of sheer incapacity, did no more than was absolutely necessary. It would have been unfair to rob the others of their laurels! Someone had to fill the pitchers, anyone could draw a cork, or even boil water. Thus, by hook or by crook, we managed to sustain life – of which the 'break' was nightly supplied to us by Howqua's coolies. They also brought (made up in bags as if 'personal effects' or 'blankets to keep off the dew,' thus passing the guards), edibles of all sorts.

"During the day we met in the Square, which became 'High Change' of experiences in desperate efforts to roast, boil or stew. Some went the length of considering it great fun; others heaped unheard of blessings upon the heads of "His Celestial Majesty", Tao-Kwang and his envoy 'Lin'."

I have also read of the younger bloods having a race to climb the greasy flag-pole, and of rat-races in the Square to while away the time. – Editor.

Basil Lubbock's Account of the War

Basil Lubbock in his book "The Opium Clippers", gives some good stories of ludicrous incidents which occurred during the war and also a graphic account of the battle for Canton.

During the Naval operations before Canton in March 1841, just before the attack started, a Chinaman came aboard the *Modeste* and asked to see "Miss-ee Kaptan". Commander Eyres took him down to his cabin where he argued on the absurdity of their fighting one another; he happened to be the Chinaman in charge of the Birdsnest Fort.

"My show you. My long yo No.1 flen. What for fightee?" he began. "Large man-ta-le [Mandarin] makee fightee, he please. Spose to-molla have got fightee, you no putee plum in you gun, my no putee plum in my gun; putee fire physic [powder] can do vellee well, makee plentee noise, makee plenty smoke. My no spillum you: you no spillum my!"

Lubbock goes on to say that when the bombardment of the Fort started, Wyres watching it through his glass, was amused to see "No. 1 good flen" with his pig-tail tied round his head.

Note on Lin Weihe

The Chinese's repeated demand for a hostage was due to a Chinaman called Lin Weihe, having been killed in a drunken brawl by British and American seamen at Hong Kong. Under Chinese Law one of the foreign seamen should have died to atone for it, but the rightful offender was never found and brought to justice – this rankled with the Chinese and gave Lin his excuse for putting on the pressure.

A Story of the *Druid*'s arrival, told by Basil Lubbock in his book "The Opium Clippers". [The American was W.H. Hunter.]

H.M.S. Druid *arrives at Macao.*
"On Jan. 24th, 1840, H.M.S. *Druid* (44 guns, Captain, the Rt. Hon. Lord John Spencer Churchill) arrived at Macao. As she was very much larger than any warship seen before in Canton waters, his Excellency Commissioner Lin and the Viceroy of Canton became more than a trifle anxious, and a mandarin was sent to the American Hong to see what he could find out."

The mandarin said: "What chance had the red-headed devils[1] in a war with the Celestial Empire, which covers the whole earth. Think of the frowning Batteries of the Hoo-Mun (the Bogue Forts). When their terrible engines are opened, the remotest corners of the world are agitated."

"Quite so," returned the American uncommitingly.

"Our Imperial Ruler controls the whole universe. His wisdom is as the five great genii, broader than the four seas in his benevolence,

---

1. *All foreigners, generally alluding to all the British.*

higher than the skies in his clemency."

"Quite so," agreed the American monotonously.

"The red-haired barbarians from a speck in the ocean come to the Flowery Land and reap unheard of money, deluging the 'Roses and Lilies' with poisonous filth. The yellow Dragon is insulted. He says: 'Drive them forth, cut them off for ever, shower upon them no longer our goodness, our tea, our rhubarb, our sweetmeats! What good to us are their buttons and musical boxes, their knives and six blades, their corkscrews and files?'"

"Quite so," droned the American.

Then at last came a tone of nervousness into the Tae-yay's speech. "A large vessel called the Too-loo-te [*Druid*] has arrived. What soldiers has she? What guns? Is it true that she carries two cannons of enormous length? – no less than 45 feet, 7 ins.? Is it true that fire-wheel ships are coming filled with flames and hot water?"

The American smiled, enjoyed frightening him, and finally let himself go saying: "Fire-wheel ships... they care not for wind and tide, they carry bombs for razing cities and wiping out forts. They eat fire and race the wind... but you will see them up the river."

Canton – the Ulster of China.

Canton, the "Ulster of China", was from the earliest days drawn into the Indo-Malayan Trade. After centuries of trade with Hindo, Parsee, and later Arab merchants, who established a settlement near Canton, it was the first Chinese seaport to be regularly visited by European traders, especially by the Portuguese who attempted to establish a monopoly, which was strenuously resisted by the Spanish, Dutch and British.

It was at this time the main outlet of the coveted Chinese production of tea, silk and rhubarb.

In the 17th century, the British made several attempts to settle at Canton, but it was not until the Portuguese monopoly was broken, that the East India Company secured a firm foothold in 1684.

The French in 1725 and the Dutch in 1762, also established Factories at Canton. From this period it became the pivot of the official policy towards foreign trade. This took the form of making Canton the sole port for foreign trade (Imperial Decree of 1707), and of the establishment of the 'Hong Concession', whereby foreign traders employed with the East India Company were confined to a special 'Factory quarter' and compelled to deal with only a small group of merchants who were directly responsible to the Imperial Government of China. The statement led to increased friction, especially when in the later 18th century, the rapid rise in the imports of Indian Opium began to alarm the Chinese authorities; and by reversing the trade balance, hitherto favourable to China, to create an international problem.

The special trade missions sent out from Great Britain under Lord Macartney (1793) and Lord Amherst (1816), both went to Peking from Canton which after the lapse of the East India Company Charter in 1854, became the Headquarters of the British Superintendent of Trade in China.

The friction soon led into the Opium Wars, which destroyed the Hong regime and substituted the Treaty Port System for it.

Chinese Edicts of 1755 and 1757.

From Research studies of the State College of Washington. "The Crucial Years of Early Anglo-Chinese Relations, 1750–1800", by Earl H. Pritchard, D.Phil., Oxon.

We learn about the Chinese Edicts of 1755 and 1757; the first one issued jointly by the Viceroy and Hoppo, which confirmed the security merchant system, established a strict monopoly of the Hong merchants, made the security merchants and linguists responsible for the acts of the supercargoes and ships officers and the two latter responsible for their men, and in general confirmed and defined in more detail the existing regulations.

The purport of the Edict was as follows:

(1) In the future, security merchants were to be Hong merchants, a "Hongist Security" was to be answerable for the duties, and

trade with the foreigners was to be conducted only by "Hongist Securities".

(2) Shopkeepers were prohibited from engaging in any kind of trade with the Europeans except in the name of "Hongist Security," and were to be organized into groups of five who were to be mutually responsible for each other.

(3) The interpreters were to obtain the permission of the "Hongist Security" before applying in his name for permission to load goods on foreign ships.

(4) In the future the "Hongist Security" and interpreter were to be responsible for any crimes committed by the supercargoes, captains, officers, and sailors, and the supercargoes and captains were to be responsible for the conduct of the sailors.

Besides being aimed at a more effective regulation of the foreigners, the Hongist monopoly were certainly a financial measure on the part of the government and officials. The security merchants had become a convenient tool for extortion from the foreigners. Officials held them responsible for all fees and dues and levied demands upon them until the merchants themselves were opposed to the system. The only way in which the Chinese traders could meet these demands was to charge the foreigners more.

In 1757, the *Onslow*[1] reached Ningpo. She was refused trade. After considerable delay, the supercargoes were informed that the Emperor did not wish foriegners to trade at Ningpo. As a result of further prolonged and fruitless negotiations, the ship sailed away with only a partial cargo, after being told that in future double duty would be charged to ships coming into Ningpo.

In the same year Ch'ien Lung issued an Edict which, together with supplementary decrees by the Viceroys of Min-che (Fukien-Chekiang) and Canton, effectively prohibited foreign trade at any Chinese port

---

1. *The Onslow was one of our ships.*

other than Canton. To insure the confinement of trade to Canton, the Emperor ordered that any European ship entering Ningpo or Chusan should surrender its arms, guns, ammunition and sails, and pay double duties. This did not absolutely prohibit trade, but the new Viceroy of Min-Che and the Viceroy of Canton issued Edicts prohibiting trade at Ningpo or Chusan and confining it to Canton.

The Royal Naval History of the War

I think at this stage an official account of what really happened in the war with China, is exceedingly interesting, so for that reason I am quoting from "The Royal Naval History", kindly lent me by the Assistant Librarian of the Royal Maritime Museum at Greenwich.

On the death of Rear-Admiral Sir Frederick Lewis Maitland K.C.B., the direction of affairs passed temporarily to the surviving senior officer on the station, Capt. Sir James, John, Gordon Bremer.

Rear-Admiral the Hon. George Elliot C.B. and Capt. Charles Elliot were appointed royal commissioners to deal with the Chinese government, the former having also the command afloat; and early in May, 1840, a squadron having on board 3,600 infantry (including H.M. 18th, 26th, and 49th Regiments), and some royal artillery and engineers, was assembled at Singapore, where, however, Rear-Admiral Elliot had not yet appeared.

In June, the squadron (then consisting of *Wellesley*, 74; *Alligator*, 28; *Conway*, 28; *Larne*, 20; *Algerine*, 10; *Rattlesnake*, 6; the two H.E.I. Co.'s steamers *Atalanta*, and *Madagascar*, and 26 transports and storeships), proceeded and, on the 21st, halted off the Great Ladrones to communicate with Macao. There Bremer declared a blockade of the Canton river, to begin on June 28th, and thence he went on to the northern harbour of Chusan, where lay a few war junks. He entered unopposed; but the local authorities, pleading lack of power to treat, refused to surrender the island. Accordingly, at 2 p.m. on July 5th, fire was opened on the Tinghae, and upon the junks; and in a few minutes the enemy was silenced, and the junks were driven ashore or reduced to wrecks. In the affair the *Wellesley*, 74, Commodore Sir James John Gordon Bremer, Capt. Thomas

Maitland; *Conway*, 28, Capt. Charles Ramsey Drinkwater Bethune, and *Algerine*, 10, and Lt. Thomas Henry Mason, took the leading parts. The town and island were then occupied, after some resistance had been offered. Ere the fighting was quite over, Rear-Admiral Elliot, in the *Melville*, 74, and Capt. the Hon Richard Saunders Dundas, arrived on the scene to assume command. In his eagerness to participate, he ran ashore his ship, then in tow of the H. East India Co.'s steamer *Atalanta*; subsequently he had to hoist his flag in the *Wellesley*, leaving the *Blenheim*, 74, Capt. Sir Humphrey Fleming Senhouse, which joined soon afterwards, to heave down the *Melville*, and to assist in repairing her.

In the meantime, letters addressed by Lord Palmerston to the advisers of the Emperor were sent in to Chinhae, at the mouth of the Ningpo River, and to Amoy. At Chinhae the communication was examined by the local mandarins, and returned as being of a nature too insulting for transmissions. At Amoy, on July 3rd., the mandarins, besides refusing to receive the message, fired treacherously on an unarmed boat the *Blonde*; whereupon Capt. Thomas Bouchier, of that frigate, opened a heavy fire and did not desist until he had reduced to silence all the works on shore. Then, leaving on the beach a copy of the letter, attached to a bamboo, he rejoined the Squadron. A blockade of the Ningpo River and the coast northward to the Yangtse Kiang was soon afterwards proclaimed; and the Rear-Admiral, with several vessels, departed to the Gulf of Péchili to negotiate. During the period of inactivity that followed, disease ravaged the Troops at Chusan, there being, between July 13th and December 31st, no fewer than 5,329 admissions to hospital, and 448 deaths there amongst the Europeans alone. It would have been wiser to employ the force to impress the Chinese with a full sense of British power; for the negotiations were prolonged, and, even while they continued, the Chinese committed further outrages, which were never properly resented and punished... The poor soldiers did not die from Chinese Canons, but from malaria, dysentry, and sand-fly fever.

At Amoy, where Com. Augustus Leopold Kuper, of the *Alligator*, 28, maintained a blockade, the threatening attitude of a large fleet of war-junks, led to the destruction of several of them, and to other reprisals. But Kuper had to abandon an attempt which he made, to force the passage between Kolangso and Amoy harbour; and consequently the Chinese were left with the conviction that they had won an important success... nowhere were they made to feel that they were dealing with foes who were vastly their superiors. Nowhere were they convincingly defeated. A truce, however, was concluded on November 6, 1840, but it was soon violated by the Chinese.

Negotiations between Capt. Elliot and the Chinese Commissioner Keeshen, dragged on until the end of the year. Elliot in *Wellesley* lay at Lintin, near the Forts of Chuenpee and the Bogue, defences of which were almost daily strengthened. The expeditionary force also, at this time, was increased, notably by the arrival of seven companies of the 7th Madras Infantry, Col. Wyndham Baker's Regiment, and the East India Company's iron steamer *Nemesis*, Master William Hutcheson Hall, R.N., "a vessel", says Ouchterlony, "destined to be very conspicuous in all the most important achievements of the war".

At length even Capt. Elliot realized that he was being trifled with, and made a laughing stock by the Chinese; and it was determined to attack the approaches to Canton. On the morning of January 7th, 1841, therefore, about 1,400 Royal Marines, and troops under Major Pratt, of the 26th Regiment, having been landed two miles south of Chuenpee Fort, pushed on against that work, while the *Calliope*, *Larne*, *Hyacinth*, *Queen* and *Nemesis* dropped anchor abreast of the batteries and opened fire. The fort was soon rushed, a landing party from the Squadron entering almost at the same moment from the sea front; and the enemy was driven away with terrible loss. On the British side the total casualties in this affair were 38 wounded...

That day the *Nemesis*, shallow of draught, well-armed, and ably handled, did wonders. After shelling Chuenpee at close range, and pouring grape into the embrasures of the fort, she pushed on over the shallows into Anson's Bay, and there attacked eleven war junks at anchor. Her first rocket directed at these set fire to the largest, which presently blew up with all on board, and, aided by boats from the Squadron, Hall soon destroyed all the others.

The works were dismantled, the guns, 97 in number, disabled, and the buildings and stores burnt. On the 8th, the Fleet, led by the *Blenheim*, 74, Capt. Sir Humphrey Fleming Senhouse, advanced to attack the Bogue Forts; but when the vessels got almost within range of Anunghoy, they were met by a Chinese emissary, bearing a request for a suspension of hostilities, and once more, accordingly, Capt. Elliott, as High Commissioner, began negotiations. He should have first razed to the ground the forts between him and Canton. On January 26th, nevertheless, he was able to announce that he had concluded a preliminary arrangement, in virtue of which Hong Kong was to be ceded to Great Britain in perpetuity, an indemnity of 86,000,000 dollars was to be paid in instalments, and official intercourse and trade were to be reopened. Hong Kong was formally taken possession of on the 26th, under a royal salute; and the Island of Chusan, at about the same time, was evacuated.

The Chinese did not keep the Treaty for long...

The *Nemesis* from "The Mariner's Mirror"

In 1840 came the never-to-be-forgotten *Nemesis*, the first iron steamer to round the Cape of Good Hope. She was an armed paddle-steamer built by Birkenhead Ironworks with 120 h.p. engines by Forrester and Co. of Liverpool and had a burden of approximately 630 tons. She left England in March 1840, under Capt. Hall, and joined the British Fleet at the Bogue Forts in November.

An officer writing aboard her on March 30th, 1841, states that she was "as much admired by our own countrymen as she was dreaded by the Chinese. Well may the latter offer a reward of 50,000 dollars for her, but she will be difficult to take. They call her the 'devil ship', and say that our shells and rockets could only be invented by the latter. They are more afraid of her than all the Line-of-Battle ships put together."

Certainly the *Nemesis* quickly appears to have earned the name of 'Nevermiss' among the British tars, and was capable of running aground with impunity. She was also unique in another sense, for although never commissioned, as one of Her Majesty's warships, she was generally commanded by officers of the Royal Navy.

Copied from the 20th. Vol of accounts and papers, 1844.

The Treaty of Nanking.
Treaty
between
HER MAJESTY
and
THE EMPEROR OF CHINA,

Signed in the English and Chinese Languages, at Nanking, August 29th, 1842. (Ratifications exchanged at Hong Kong, June 26th, 1843.)

Her Majesty the Queen of the United Kingdom of Great Britain and Ireland, and His Majesty the Emperor of China, being desirous of putting an end to the misunderstandings and consequent hostilities which have arisen between the two countries, have resolved to conclude a Treaty for that purpose, and have therefore named as their Plenipotentiaries, that is to say:-

Her Majesty the Queen of Great Britain and Ireland, Sir Henry Pottinger, Bart., a Major-General in the service of the East India Co. etc., etc.

And His Imperial Majesty the Emperor of China, the High Commissioners Keying, a Member of the Imperial House, a Guardian of the Crown Prince, and General of the garrison of Canton; and Elepoo, of the Imperial Kindred, graciously permitted to wear the insignia of the first rank, and the distinction of the peacock's feather, lately Minister and Governor-General etc. and now Lt. General commanding at Chapoo;

Who, after having communicated to each other their respective Full Powers, and found them to be in good and due form, have agreed upon and concluded the following Articles:-

ARTICLE I

There shall henceforward be Peace and Friendship between Her Majesty the Queen of the United Kingdom of Great Britain and Ireland and His Majesty the Emperor of China, and between their respective subjects, who shall enjoy full security and protection for their persons and property within the dominions of the other.

ARTICLE II

His Majesty the Emperor of China agrees, that British subjects, with their families and establishments, shall be allowed to reside, for the purpose of carrying on their mercantile pursuits, without molestation or restraint, at the cities and towns of Canton, Amoy, Roochowfoo, Ningpo, and Shanghai; and Her Majesty the Queen of Great Britain etc., will appoint Superintendents, or Consular Officers, to reside at each of the above-named cities or towns, to be the medium of communication between the Chinese authorities and the said merchants, and to see that the just duties and other dues of the Chinese Government, as hereafter provided for, are duly discharged by Her Brittanic Majesty's subjects.

ARTICLE III

It being obviously necessary and desirable that British subjects should have some port whereat they may careen and refit their ships when required, and keep stores for that purpose, His Majesty the Emperor of China ceded to Her Majesty the Queen of Great Britain etc., the Island of Hong Kong, to be possessed in perpetuity by Her Britannick Majesty, her Heirs and Successors, and to be governed by such laws and regulations as Her Majesty the Queen of Great Britain etc., shall see fit to direct.

ARTICLE IV

The Emperor of China agrees to pay the sum of six millions of dollars, as the value of the Opium which was delivered up at Canton in the month of March, 1839, as a ransom for the lives of Her Britannick Majesty's Superintendent and subjects, who had been imprisoned and threatened with death by the Chinese High Officers.

ARTICLE V

The Government of China having compelled the British merchants trading at Canton, to deal exclusively with certain Chinese merchants, called Hong merchants (or Co-Hong), who had been licensed by the Chinese Government for that purpose, the Emperor of

China agrees to abolish the practise in future at all ports where British merchants may reside, and to permit them to carry on their mercantile transactions with whatever persons they please; and His Imperial Majesty further agrees to pay to the British Government the sum of three millions of dollars, on account of debts due to British subjects by some of the said Hong Merchants or Co-Hong, who have become insolvent, and who owe very large sums of money as subjects ot her Britannick Majesty.

ARTICLE VI

The Government of Her Britannick Majesty having been obliged to send out an Expedition to demand and obtain redress for the violent and unjust proceedings of the Chinese High Authorities toward Her Britannick Majesty's officer and subjects, the Emperor of China agrees to pay the sum of 12 millions of dollars, on account of their having resided under, the expenses incurred; and Her Britannick Majesty's Plenipotentiary voluntarily agrees, on behalf of Her Majesty, to deduct from the said amount of twelve millions of dollars, any sums which may have been received by Her Majesty's combined Forces, as ransom for cities and towns in China, subsequent to the 1st day of August, 1841.

ARTICLE VII

It is agreed, that the total amount of twenty-one millions of dollars, described in the three proceeding Articles, shall be paid as follows:-

Six millions immediately.

Six millions in 1843; that is, three millions on or before the 30th of the month of June, and three millions on or before the 31st of December.

Five millions in 1844; that is, two millions on or before the 30th of June, and two millions on or before the 31st of December.

And it is further stipulated, that interest, at the rate of 5 per cent. per annum, shall be paid by the Government of China on any portion of the above sums that are not punctually discharged at the periods fixed.

ARTICLE VIII

The Emperor of China agrees to release unconditionally all subjects of Her Britannick Majesty (whether natives of Europe or India), who may be in confinement at this moment in any part of the Chinese Empire.

ARTICLE IX

The Emperor of China agrees to publish and promulgate, under His Imperial Sign Manual and Seal, a full and entire amnesty and act of indemnity to all subjects of China, on account of their having resided under, or having had dealings and intercourse with, or having entered the service of Her Britannick Majesty, or of Her Majesty's Officers, and His Imperial Majesty further engages to release all Chinese subjects who may be at this moment in confinement for similar reasons.

ARTICLE X

His Majesty the Emperor of China agrees to establish at all ports which are, by the Second Article of this Treaty, to be thrown open for the resort of British Merchants, a fair and regular Tariff of export and import customs and other dues, which Tariff shall be publicly notified and promulgated for general information; and the Emperor further engages, that when British merchandize shall have once paid at any of the said ports the regulated customs and dues, agreeable to the Tariff to be hereafter fixed, such merchandize may be conveyed by Chinese merchants to any province or city in the interior of the Empire of China, on paying a further amount as transit duties, which shall not exceed 5 per cent on the Tariff value of such goods.

ARTICLE XI

It is agreed that Her Britannick Majesty's Chief High Officer in China shall correspond with the Chinese High Officers, both at the capital and in the Provinces, under the term 'communications' (Chinese sign); with the subordinate British Officers and Chinese High Officers in the Provinces, under the terms 'statement' (Chinese sign) on the part of the former, and on the part of the latter, 'declaration' (Chinese sign); and the sub-ordinates of both countries on a footing of perfect equality; merchants and others not holding official situations, and therefore not included in the above, on both sides, to use the term 'representation' (Chinese sign) in all papers addressed to, or intended for the notice of, the respective Governments.

ARTICLE XII

On the assent of the Emperor of China to this Treaty being received, and the discharge of the first instalment of money, Her Britannick Majesty's forces will retire from Nanking and the Grand Canal, and will no longer molest or stop the trade of China. The military post at Chinhai will also be withdrawn; but the islands of Koolangoo, and that of Chusan, will continue to be held by Her Majesty's forces until the money payments, and the arrangements for opening the ports to British merchants, be completed.

ARTICLE XIII

The Ratification of this Treaty by Her Majesty the Queen of Great Britain etc., and His Majesty the Emperor of China, shall be exchanged as soon as the great distance which separates England from China will admit; but in the meantimes, counterpart copies of it, signed and sealed by the Plenipotentiaries on behalf of their respective Sovereigns, shall be mutually delivered, and all its provisions and arrangements shall take effect.

Done at Nanking, and signed and sealed by the Plenipotentiaries on board Her Britannic Majesty's ship *Cornwallis*, this twenty-ninth day of August, 1842; corresponding with the Chinese date, twenty-fourth day of the seventh month, in the twenty-second year of Taoukwang.

(L.S.) HENRY POTTINGER

Her M.'s Plenipotentiary.

Seal of the Chinese
High
Commissioner.

Signature of 3rd. Chinese Plenipotentiary.	Signature of 2nd. Chinese Plenipotentiary.	Signature of 1st. Chinese Plenipotentiary.

The Story of the Founding of the East India Company.

In the 17th and 18th centuries, East India Companies were established by Holland, Denmark, Scotland, Austria and Sweden... The English Company was founded at the end of the 16th Century in order to compete with Dutch merchants, who had obtained a practical monopoly of the trade with the Spice Islands and had raised the price of pepper from 3/- to 8/- per lb. Queen Elizabeth incorporated it by Royal Charter, dated December 31st, 1600, under the title of "The Governor and Company of Merchants of London, trading with the East Indies." The Charter conferred the sole right of trading with the East Indies – i.e. with all countries lying beyond the Cape of Good Hope or the Straits of Magellan – upon the Company for a term of 15 years. Unauthorized interlopers were liable to forfeiture of ships and cargo. There were 125 shareholders in the original East India Company with a capital of £72,000... the early voyages reached as far as Japan... In 1609 James I renewed the Company's Charter "for ever." ...Meanwhile friction was arising between English and Dutch Companies. The Dutch traders considered that they had prior rights in the Far East.

The need for good ships for the East India Trade had led the Company in 1609 to construct the dockyard at Deptford, from which, as Monson observes, dates "the increase of great ships in England". Down to the middle of the 19th century, the famous "East Indiamen" held unquestioned pre-eminence among the merchant vessels of the world. Throughout the 17th century they had to be prepared at any moment, to fight, not merely Malay pirates, but the armed trading vessels of their Dutch, French, and Portuguese rivals...

In the reign of Charles II, it grew, from a single trading Company – to use the modern term – with the right to acquire territory, coin money, command fortresses and troops, form alliances, make war and peace, and exercise both civil and criminal jurisdiction. It is accordingly in 1689, when the three presidencies of Bengal, Madras and Bombay had lately been established, that the ruling career of the East India Company begins.

In 1784, Pitt's India Bill created a Board of Control, as a department of the English government to exercise political, military, and financial superintendence over the British possessions in India. ...From this date the direction of Indian policy passed definitely from the Company to the Governor-General in India, and the Ministry in London... The monopoly of valuable trade with China, chiefly in tea, was ended by Earl Grey's Act of 1833. Its property was then secured on the Indian possession and its annual dividends of ten guineas per £100 Stock were made a charge upon the Indian revenue. Henceforth the East India Company ceased to be a trading concern and exercised only administrative functions. Such a position could not, in the nature of things, be permanent, and the Indian Mutiny was followed by the entire transference of Indian administation to the Crown on August 2nd, 1858.

From the Encyclopedia Britannica.

Bibliography

AUTHOR	TITLE	PUBLISHER
Clagette BLAKE	Charles Elliot, R.N. 1801–1875	London, Cleaver Hume Press Ltd.
E. BACKHOUSE & J.O. BLAND	Annals & Memoirs of the Court of Peking	London, William Heinemann, 1914.
William H. BRERETON	The Truth about Opium	London, W.H. Allen & Co, 13 Waterloo Place, London, 1882.
Hsin-Pao CHANG	Commissioner Lin and the Opium Wars	Harvard University Press, 1964, & distrib. Oxford University Press.
Maurice COLLIS	Foreign Mud	Faber & Faber Ltd, 24 Russell Square, London.
CORDIER	Bibliotica Sinica	
W.C. COSTIN, M.A.	Great Britain & China, 1833–60	Oxford, Clarendon Press, 1937.
Sir U. CUMMING	Political India, 1832–1932	A Co-operative survey of the Century, 1932
Raymond DAWSON	The Legacy of China	Oxford, Clarendon Press, 1964.
Henry DODWELL	The Nabobs of Madras	London, Williams & Norgate Ltd., 14 Henrietta Street, Covent Garden, London, W.C.2.
Janet DUNBAR	Golden Interlude	London, A.D. Innes & Co., Bedford Street, 1895.
Emily ELDEN's DIARIES		Seen in the original India Office.
Robert S. ELEGANT	The Centre of the World	London, Methuen & Co. Ltd., 36 Essex St., W.C.2.

Grace FOX	British Admirals & Chinese Pirates 1832–1869	Routledge & Kegan Paul Ltd.
Edgar HOLT	The Opium Wars in China	Putnam, 42 Russell Street, London.
William C. HUNTER	The 'Fan Kwae' at Canton before Treaty Days 1825–1844	Kelly and Walsh Ltd, Shanghai, Hongkong, Singapore, & Yokohama.
Basil LUBBOCK	The Opium Clippers	Brown, Son & Ferguson, Ltd., 52 Darnley Street, Glasgow, S.1.
H.B. MORSE & H.F. MacNAIR	Far Eastern International Relations	Houghton, Mifflin Co. Boston, N.Y., Chicago, Atlanta, San Francisco and Riverside Press, Cambridge.
E.T.C. WERNER	Chinese Weapons	N. China Branch Royal Asiatic Soc. Shanghai or 56 Queen Street, London.
Cecil WOODHAM SMITH	The Reason Why	Constable & Co., London.
J.K. STANFORD	Ladies in the Sun	J.M. Dent & Son, London.

Final Note

When my husband first went out to Egypt in 1912, his career was in the Egyptian Civil Service, and to qualify for this he had to do a fourth year at Oxford in which to learn Arabic, in which he became very fluent. To start with he worked as a kind of country magistrate settling village disputes. If it was nearby he rode a horse, if it was far away he rode a motor bicycle, which the villagers called "the white man's tin donkey!"

He told me that he occasionally came across a Maria Theresa dollar in the Sudan, something like our old 5/- piece I think. The other kind of silver the Chinese liked was Sycee silver: small lumps of solid silver shaped like a Chinese woman's tiny shoe, and very carefully weighed by the Shroff and stamped with his mark. When these forms of silver came to an end the Chinese demanded opium.

So, as tea drinking became more and more popular in England, we needed more and more opium; so we grew it in India and shipped it to Canton to pay for the tea.

So, though we may have been denigrated for selling opium to the Chinese, it was not really our fault. Wyndham mentions in one of his letters that they had started growing tea in Assam, but it would take some time before it could be sold.

The Editor.